2024

The Exploratory Mind

Rewiring Sentience

Aimon Kopera, MD

ISBN: 979-8-9893545-2-8

Published in the United States of America by
Qi Mountain Press
2525 Main Street, Suite 110
Santa Monica, CA 90405
Phone 424.527.6009
www.qimountain.com

For All Sentience

CONTENTS

Praise

"Dr. Kopera steps far outside the boundaries of her conventional medical training to dive into the magical, mysterious, mystical and healing dimensions of the possibility for a life of profound transformation. Leaving no spiritual stone unturned, she invites the reader to intimately join her on a decades-long quest to experience the hidden depth of our shared existence on this often difficult-to-navigate ordeal: a human life."

~ Eliezer Sobel, author of *The 99th Monkey: A Spiritual Journalist's Misadventures With Gurus, Messiahs, Sex, Psychedelics and Other Consciousness-Raising Experiments*

"Dr. Kopera has written a beautiful book. It is a piece of unique art. It transports we the readers to exotic places in the world and in our minds and spirits. What a wonderful set of short stories which act as windows into a wide variety of ways to expand our consciousness."

~ Jeffery M. Fletcher, Artist and Author of *Looking Back an Artists Perspective*

"Dr Aimon wrote a captivating book which leads people into lands of possibilities and ways to expand our views of existence. It is a healing book which led me to consider paths and tools I had not encountered nor considered. It is a joyous celebration of life a human transformation."

~ Michael Peter Langevin, Author of *Travel Tales from Unknown Realities*

"A great read for those who like adventure. Not adventure as in the Indiana Jones films, but if Indiana Jones was exploring his mind and consciousness. Dr. Kopera does go to exotic locales for her explorations – Thailand (where she was born), Cambodia, Peru, India, Portugal, Jamaica, and America-- not as a tourist or an explorer of exotic locales, but as an explorer of perception and meaning. Sometimes the adventures incorporate mind-opening substances, all of them approached with great intelligence and heart. A fascinating read."

~ Bill Russel, Author and Director of *the Broadway play Side Show* ...

"*The Exploratory Mind, Rewiring Sentience,* is a profound and humbling read. Doctor Kopera writing style is warm pulling you into the heart of the story, allowing you to *feel* her experiences from the inside out. She explores our primordial roots emerging from cosmic forces expressed in the complexity of human incarnation, giving us context, posing questions, and offering means of exploration. Ranging from plant-based therapies—psychedelics and not —meditation, profound silence, darkness, mindful movement, and detoxification strategies for the subtle and physical. Perhaps the most beautiful aspect is her gently guiding us back to curiosity as the ebb and pulse of evolution. I can honestly say this is a life changing read!"

~ Candice Covington, author of *Vibrational Nutrition: Understanding the Energetic Signature of Foods*

"This book tells the story of a doctor from Thailand and her extraordinary research into practices and psychoactive chemicals known to heal, elevate, and transform human consciousness. From a prolonged retreat in total darkness to adventures with ayahuasca and remote viewing, she recounts her own numerous explorations into the mysteries of mind and brain, intent on creating a new and more inspiring paradigm of human flourishing. A pleasure to read, highly recommended. "

~ Michael Grosso, PHD, author of *Frontiers of the Soul: Exploring Psychic Evolution*

"*The Exploratory Mind* is a compelling and highly entertaining account of one person's journey through expanded awareness. The author's practical, matter-of-fact approach to deepening her psychic abilities as she participated in many different schools of consciousness development is especially encouraging to those readers who are just starting out on the spiritual path, who are often nagged by doubts about both the path underfoot and their own ability to follow it. Some of the practices which the author describes I, too, have pursued (such as the teachings and techniques of Mantak Chia, indigenous shamanism, and psychedelics); and I found her take on these subjects to be illuminating and helpful. In particular, there is a chapter on the subject of Gratitude, which to me sums up the entire essence of the spiritual path. *The Exploratory Mind* is a valuable guide to the many different avenues of psychic training which are available to the dedicated seeker."

~ Bob Makransky, author of *Magical Living*

"Dear and Precious SpiritSoul that You Are, amazing work is being offered here for anyone who chooses to explore and benefit from having safe and natural extraordinary and altered states of consciousness without the use of substances. These extraordinary states of mind and consciousness offer wonderful and meaningful experiences within one's self and available to everyone who is willing to venture beyond the ordinary and mundane world-programmed reality. Dr. Aimon Kopera has explored, starting with meditation and then each of these processes, exercises, and meditations she so generously has compiled and made available for our benefit.

This knowledge provides step by step guidance to open doors of perception to explore, and utilize in our daily activities and affairs, life's work/dharma, and relationships, especially with one's inner wisdom, protector and maintainer. With Dr. Kopera as a genuine healing facilitator who, in my opinion, knows how important "physician heal thyself" and to be a living example of what she offers to others.

I feel this work gives us sincerity, inner desire, and intention, the very tools that each one of us can use for his or her own self-realization and navigate the rough waters of this basically mental reality, enjoy the ride, and be able to access inner strength, wisdom, and guidance from one's authentic self."

~ Terry Cole-Whittaker DD, author of *What You Think of Me is None of My Business*

"In *The Exploratory Mind,* Dr. Aimon Kopra takes us through a journey, ranging from the power of gratitude to possibilities of the spiritual uses of various psychedelic drugs, to an extended darkness retreat, culminating in a fire walk and a feeling of rebirth. Drawing on her experiences at the Monroe Institute, remote viewing, including The Matrix Field – as she calls it - the all

-pervasive cosmic web that connects every form of life and consciousness across space and time.

The above barely scratches the surface of the book's many topics, so let me conclude by saying that this is indeed a spiritual journey that is a most interesting and worthwhile read."

~ Bob Frissell, author of *Catching the Ascension Wave*

"Join Dr. Aimon Kopera on a sacred journey of her visions, life experiences, deep service and transformation that reveal many pathways to consciousness, healing, spiritual connection and personal growth.

Each chapter and story ignites different perspectives into so many multi-cultural and community modalities of spiritual and medicinal disciplines to awaken realms of consciousness.

The Exploratory Mind is a heartfelt, deeply powerful and moving exploration of life experiences that illuminate, inspire and create new ways of thinking, being, doing and celebrating life."

~ Lumari, author of *Streams of Consciousness*

"The author's own exploration brought her to Machu Picchu where she precariously lay outside down on an oval-shaped stone "teetering on the brink of a plunge" into oblivion. This is emblematic of the journey she offers the reader to see the world "unfettered by the usual bounds of perspective." A bold and mind-altering flight for the "condors" of our world."

~ John Nelson, author of *Threshold* and *A Guide to Energetic Healing*

"The Exploratory Mind by Dr. Aimon Kopera was an insightful and fascinating read, especially the chapters about The Monroe Institute and remote viewing. This is a book which explores many ways to expand the mind and spirit. Dr Kopera has traveled the world researching many possible methods of self-improvement and consciousness exploration. She writes about them in a captivating fashion and explains them in a way that I think will make them approachable for any person curious about the vast potential of our minds."

~Andrea Berger, author of *Quantum Healing with the Biofeedback L.I.F.E. System* co author of You are More than your Physical Body. (A Monroe Institute trainer).

"*The Exploratory Mind* is a uniquely inspiring memoir, a wealth of insight and wisdom gleaned from over three decades of courageous consciousness exploration, using various methods, techniques, and psychedelic sacraments. Drawing from her medical background and multi-cultural heritage, Aimon Kopera masterfully integrates timeless knowledge from ancient traditions with contemporary science and shares her extensive personal experience exploring the transformative power, therapeutic benefits, and untapped potential that non-ordinary states of mind have for spiritual growth and healing. Beautifully written, *The Exploratory Mind* serves as both a map and a compass, helping us to navigate our own inner journeys. Most highly recommended!"

~David Jay Brown, author of *Dreaming Wide Awake* and *The New Science of Psychedelics*

"Although she doesn't quite say it, reading, Exploratory mind I felt Dr, Kopera was looking at our connection with God or the divine from any different perspectives. The book is captivating, inspiring and fun."

~Brian McCure, author of *Who Am I?*

"Reading The Exploratory Mind, I felt Dr Aimon Kopera has danced with the Devine Architect. She understands the essence of UFO like phenomena. This book offers personal insights into expanding and adventuring in mind and spirit."

~Robert Perala, author of *The Divine Architect: The Art of Living and Beyond*

"The magic in life can be approached in many ways along many paths. This book explores some extreme ones. Dr. Kopera and her adventures are beyond entertaining, they reach the level of transcendent."

~Sirona Knight, author of *Dream Magic: Night Spells and Rituals for Love, Prosperity and Personal Power*

"The Exploratory Mind is an amazing collection of alternative reality experiences written by, Dr Aimon Kopera, who is a medical doctor, who owns her own clinic. Many who have been curious about these adventures that they may have heard about will find this: extremely useful. It is beautifully written and is very easy to read. This is an armchair book that looks into the world of alternative spiritual experiences. I highly recommend this book."

~Maureen J St Germain, author of: *Waking up in 5 D* and *The Akashic Record*

"This exciting book is a testament to what can happen when somebody gets past fear and opens themselves to a vividly alive hidden world. We are in the process of entering a new era of relationship between humanity and what I personally regard as another, equally complex but more vivid consciousness that exists among plants. It is a carefully drawn, inspirational and responsible testament to what a relationship with this other consciousness has to offer us, which is a new way of living, being and understanding."

~Whitley Strieber, author of *Communion*

"*The Exploratory Mind* is a fascinating book. It inspires us all to reconsider the limits of our minds. Dr. Aimon Kopera is bold, intelligent, and adventurous, and her writing style makes the concepts easily accessible."

~Steven Halpern, Grammy ® nominated musician and OG Sound Healer

"In *The Exploratory Mind: Rewiring Sentience,* Dr Aimon Kopera speaks from the powerful intention to hold "a lantern aloft" for humanity, as we evolve toward our collective healing. An intrepid Way Shower, she chronicles her journey into non-ordinary realities, seeking "the role of the mind and consciousness in self-healing."

Dr Kopera is expertly qualified to analyze a wide variety of spiritual practices and approaches that serve to foster enlightenment and healing. She explains the benefits and safety precautions involved in the rewiring and repairing of the human psyche, whether by means of traditional spiritual practices or the use of psychedelic-assisted therapies. Thank you, Dr. Kopera, for a truly inspiring message to the world, envisioning healing that reaches from individuals to society at large, and beyond, even to an end to "the pattern of war!"

~Karen S Mitchell, Social Ecologist, Earth Keeper, writer in *The Echo World: The Alternative Voice for Spiritual and Cultural Creatives*

Preface

From my early years, perhaps as far back as secondary school, I've felt an unyielding urge to share my narrative—a profound connection to a higher self that found me in heartfelt conversations with the moon and stars. For years, this inner calling lay dormant, awaiting the perfect moment to manifest. Now, having embarked on this literary journey, I see this text as a destined path that has culminated from my joyous exploration of existence.

Fueled by the kaleidoscope of experiences that my life offers, I wish to convey that living fully is within everyone's grasp. My aim is to encourage you to embrace the entirety of your being, and to assure you that you are perennially supported in your quest for self-fulfillment and achievement.

As you traverse the landscapes of this book, my hope is that it serves as a catalyst for growth and understanding. This is not a solitary expedition but a collective undertaking. Driven by love and a commitment to foster healing, the book extends an invitation to everyone, encouraging both individual and communal growth.

In addition to my professional trajectory, my soul's adventurous yearnings have led me into awe-inspiring realms far removed from the ordinary. Over three decades, an unquenchable curiosity about the intricate dimensions of life, death, and the cosmos has woven a vibrant tapestry of unparalleled experiences. It is these experiences that I am so eager to share with the world.

At this heart of the book is the principle that life's events unfold in serendipitous synchronicity, often culminating in profound "aha" moments. The book is meant to serve as a compass, guiding you through the complex choreography that leads to your own revelations.

The very act of writing has ushered me into an extraordinary mental landscape. Following intense bouts of recalling, research, and verification, I experience a euphoric clarity devoid of any external influence, as if my body's own DMT kicks in nightly. This has intensified my resolve, sharpened my focus, and opened the floodgates for unrestrained information flow.

Beyond writing, my pursuits are many. Marrying my credentials as a medical doctor with an avid interest in the frontiers of mind, consciousness, psychedelics, and ethnobotanical medicine, I blend ancient traditions with contemporary science to shepherd people into transformative states of awareness. This zeal for cognitive metamorphosis and self-discovery has catapulted me onto global platforms as a sought-after speaker. I've ventured into the sacred sanctuaries of over a hundred countries, orchestrating transformative expeditions that ignite healing and cultivate personal growth.

Each morning, I attune to the whispered wisdom of the dawn, the sun, and the sky, living a life imbued with joy, serenity, and unpretentious elegance. As twilight descends, I eagerly anticipate the night's slumber, a sojourn that permits travel into other realms of consciousness and serves as an inward voyage to cleanse the experiences of the day. I do not expect (nor want) anyone to take routines like these and enforce them upon themselves because they "should". Instead, I hope to inspire you to discover routines and practices that feed your soul directly.

My writing was largely motivated by a sense of urgency to awaken and guide those ready to embark on their own extraordinary life journeys. Informed by the existential recognition that we are spiritual entities having a finite human experience, I adopt the role of a vigilant observer. I have chronicled the compelling stories of my time, with the ultimate goal of engendering inner peace and profound joy in others.

As I take on the mantle of a guide, I look forward with eagerness to forming resonant connections with those open to navigating the complex, rewarding path of self-discovery and personal growth.

This book is a lantern held aloft for the seekers among us—those standing at the threshold of an unparalleled journey into the depths of their own essence. While the musings and observations presented herein may not universally resonate, they aim to serve as a guiding light for those poised to delve into expanded self-awareness and ascend to new heights of consciousness.

It's my aspiration that, in reading this, you will walk away with the liberating epiphany that the power to recast your life in alignment with your deepest yearnings lies inherently within you. This transformation involves a mindful allowance for neuroplasticity—a willing surrender to the expansive realm of human experience. While the metamorphosis may not unfold instantly, my hope is that, at some critical juncture, you will experience an awakening—whatever that word may mean to you.

I invite you to relinquish your preconceived notions and egoistic barriers, thus creating room for the extraordinary states of being that await you in these pages. I am profoundly grateful for this serendipitous meeting between you and this body of work. As you turn each page, may you unearth deep-seated connections and revelatory insights, unlocking the untapped reservoirs of your own limitless potential.

Three Weeks in the Dark

Screams ripped through the abyss…

…probably not the first thing that comes to mind when thinking of spirituality or meditation—but if there is one key lesson that could be translated out of my three-week night, it's that you cannot have enlightenment without darkness. Whether you think of it as a key, a doorway, or a rite of passage, time spent in the dark is something to be valued. That is exactly why I decided to seek it out.

It was 2002 and, at the time, Tao Darkness Retreat was not only the best darkness retreat available; it was the only one. Already, it was known as an advanced practice, meaning that the experience could be so intense that only those who had spent decades cultivating a still and expansive mind were advised to attend. Anyone who was not properly prepared would likely come face to face with some kind of personal demon in the dark. When we meet our own personal demons, it represents a healing process. Some need more healing than others. It also represents our own resistance to the process of learning and growth. Without a doubt, some participants in the darkness retreat encountered demons that they were not ready to learn about.

Hence, the screaming.

This was why the retreat had a strict buddy system. It was a matter of safety comparable to scuba diving. If there is a malfunction with your breathing apparatus, you need someone there to help you. In the case of darkness, your breathing apparatus is consciousness itself. The comparison to diving into a vast ocean full of life was apt in many ways, and only served to draw me in.

I was living in Greenville, South Carolina, and well-established as a businesswoman, social entrepreneur, and spiritual guide. My pride and joy was a wellness center, the first of its kind in the area, where people could heal, create, and use technology to achieve different levels of consciousness. My love of the wellness process made me a very hands-on owner,

In my stead, I asked two people to fill-in for me. My assistant Mary was familiar with the wellness center, and my manager Lesa was familiar with running a business. I knew that once I was in the dark, I had to be confident and at ease regarding the affairs I had left behind. Mary and Lesa were the best possible people to deliver that peace.

This idea of leaving things behind is, understandably, something that prevents many people from having experiences like the one I was heading into. Employment and parenthood are difficult things to leave behind. For some, though, the primary obstacle is more mental than logistical. Setting aside weeks at a time for personal growth and spiritual excursions can be challenging. We often create responsibilities that tie us down to certain patterns, establishing common paradigms that prevent us from experiencing what we truly desire.

I faced that challenge as well, because my pattern thus far had been one of constantly doing, having, and being entangled in various creations and projects. We all have this in one way or another—the fear of putting our lives on hold, or feeling as though they are stagnant for three whole weeks.

The cure for this feeling is to realize that a retreat of such spiritual growth is not holding life back, but launching it forward. It all comes down to the choices we make and the actions we choose to prioritize. If we value spiritual growth, then that importance will be reflected in different aspects of our lives.

In secret, some people might have thought I was crazy for taking this journey. Some were curious about how I managed to do it. Others told me they wished they could. Still, others mentioned that if given three full weeks to explore life, they would prefer to do so in the light. It's a preference that I certainly could not criticize, as there is much to be found in the light. But, as I was about to discover, the darkness also has so much to offer.

Sensory deprivation was merely the tip of the iceberg. Subjecting the human body to such prolonged periods of darkness had very real, biochemical effects. It causes the release of what's called a spirit molecule in more mystical settings. For science and medicine, it is a neurotransmitter known as DMT.

Those who are familiar with psychoactive substances may recognize this chemical from its presence in Ayahuasca. When consumed, it alters the user's state of consciousness, often causing experiences like ascending to a higher spiritual plane.

Our bodies can synthesize and release various neurotransmitters depending on our needs. You may be familiar with tryptophan, serotonin, or melatonin. All of these are neurotransmitters that regulate aspects of our state of mind including mood, cognition, behavior, appetite, and sleep.

Our bodies have an innate ability to produce these substances, and DMT is no exception. It is frequently released when we die, but its creation can also be triggered by, you guessed it, prolonged exposure to darkness.

Every neurotransmitter has its own unique effect, and DMT affects our sensory perception and cognition. As you can imagine, dialing up visual perception and memory can result in a quite detailed trip down memory lane, which can be pleasant and insightful but, I'll say it again:

Hence, the screaming.

This is why in the three weeks leading up to the retreat, I doubled my standard meditation practice to cultivate an extremely positive mindset. When people hear the word positive, they naturally think of things like "good" or "happy," but this is not exactly the kind of mindset I was pursuing. To me, positive means you are in a state of expansion, whereas negative is contraction. Both states are as natural and necessary as the very act of breathing.

When positive, our minds are loose, comfortable, and eager to explore, even if that exploration brings sadness. This was the state of mind that I wanted to inhabit in the dark—not to be happy, fearless, and never feel the urge to scream myself. Instead, if some kind of pain happened to surface, I wouldn't look at it as a failure, but an opportunity to explore.

As one final step of preparation, I completed a 72-hour fast, which helped me to purify, and to find physical and emotional grounding. With that, once life at home was buttoned-up, I packed my things and made my way to Northern Thailand, where the retreat was located.

I had so many questions. On the fundamental level, I simply wanted to know what the mind is. Is it a thinking machine, or a thinking system? By that I mean, is the mind something that is influenced by thinking, or is it the thinking itself? How does it work? None of these were answers I could hope to have answered in words, but I hoped I could come closer to some understanding of this miraculous force that made me who I am.

From the outside, the facility appeared almost to be a perfect cube, a two-stories tall and made of brick and wood. The interior, well, I never saw it. There was no tour given with lights on for us to familiarize ourselves with the layout of the space that we would soon be blindly navigating. That sense of mystery was an important part of the retreat's design.

One of the foundational pillars of the experience was

trust, the willingness to enter the unknown and explore it for yourself. If people were to see the space in advance and make assessments based on the critical sight of the mind, they would be missing out on a huge opportunity. The analytical part of your mind that craves detail must be quelled so you can surrender yourself to the unknown.

These were all ideas that I found very exciting, so much so that I was the only member of the group who had requested to have the experience without obliging the buddy system. I had been working to still my mind and cultivate a positive mindset since I was a child.

I grew up as part of a unique blend of cultures, traditions, and philosophies. Being of half-Chinese and half-Thai descent, I was raised in a multicultural tapestry in Bangkok, a city that was both sprawling and intimate, traditional and progressive.

From the age of seven or eight, my curiosity led me to Lumphini Park, a vibrant microcosm of life. At the center of the park, there was a big lake, surrounded by beautiful lush trees and tropical flowers. The whole area was like a refuge for wildlife in the heart of the city. Similar to Central Park in New York, this park was a sanctuary within the city, a serene retreat where the elderly, the young, and everyone in between found a space to unwind, to express, and to meditate.

Intrigued by the graceful movements of many groups there, I began my journey into the realms of Tai Chi and Qigong. I was drawn to the park day after day, the novelty of the exercise captivating my young mind.

Growing up in Bangkok was like navigating an intricately patterned mosaic, a mixture of history, modernity, and diverse ethnicities. In the midst of this vibrancy, I found myself drawn towards my Chinese heritage. My family had immigrated to Thailand, adopting the land as their own, a phenomenon that perhaps was uniquely possible there given Thailand's history of never having been colonized. As opposed to the policy of many western nations, the Thai government had welcomed Chinese immigrants, fostering a sense of unity and respect for cultural diversity.

The allure of the Thai-Chinese culture was powerful. The industriousness of the Chinese immigrants and their dedication to the wellbeing of the next generation deeply resonated with me. Their practices, beliefs, and traditions shaped my childhood, nurturing my interest in Chinese yoga, Tai Chi, and Qigong.

The park was a significant aspect of my childhood, and I had no way of knowing that, it was an early training ground for my mind to not only withstand, but indeed thrive, in twenty-one days of darkness. Its locale on a historic road, with roots tracing back to the 1930s and 1940s, added to its charm. The park was an open invitation for all – the young, the elderly, residents, and tourists. As I ventured into the park, I was greeted by groups of people engaged in fan dancing, Tai Chi, and martial arts – an enchanting symphony of movement and mindfulness. This was a community that transcended my family, a larger familial structure that nourished and guided me.

One of the most memorable aspects of my childhood

was joining a Tai Chi group. In the park, under the wise tutelage of an old Chinese man with a classic long white beard, I learned and practiced Tai Chi and the fan dance— specifically known as Praying Mantis, practiced since ancient times.

I was a child who loved to explore, to understand, to assist others. I was drawn towards helping people, whether they were beggars on the streets or elderly individuals struggling to walk. I found joy in making others happy, and this, in turn, sparked a sense of fulfillment within me.

This was a launchpad, a simple starting point for a mindset and lifestyle that would carry through into my adult life. With all this experience, I felt comfortable asking the retreat's master, Mantak Chia, for permission to enter the darkness alone.

My mental state was grounded, clear, I had no history of a mental disorder, and Mantak Chia knew all of this because we had worked together in the past. So, he allowed me as an exception to their strict buddy system policy—I would be going in alone.

As we entered, I was brimming with excitement and curiosity. The retreat space was shielded from light by three layers of rooms, which worked like airlocks. We entered the first small room, closed the door behind us before opening the one ahead, then repeated the process.

Once we were truly inside, we could only interpret the place by touch, scent, and the way that our voices reverberated off of the walls. The details I sensed immediately painted a picture in my mind. The main common area was wide open, the ceiling was high, and most of the construction was made of wood. Of course, I will never know the retreat's true interior design, but I could *feel* an earth-tone color pallet.

Master Mantak Chia, a renowned Taoist master, introduced us to the layout of the space. The first floor was a wide-open hall for meditation, Tai chi, Qigong, and Taoist yoga . There, we listened to the master's teachings and received essential instructions and were provided with our schedule. Each event on the daily schedule would be marked by the gentle strike of a gong.

The first would be at 5 AM, signaling that participants were welcome to get up and meditate in their rooms, or in the meditation hall. The second bell sounded at 6 AM, indicating that fruit and juice were available at the food area for those who wanted to eat. Then, at 8 AM, the master would lead us in group meditation. Participants were free to be comfortable in their own space and engage in their self-process, maintain silence, or be in close contact with the group.

The following bell would sound at noon, more for the sake of tracking time than anything. At 5 PM, an evening meal was signaled and finally, 8 PM would be what other retreats called "lights out." For us, it was simply "silence."

That first day had some similarities to other retreats. Everyone settled into their personal spaces and bonded over the uniqueness of the experience thus far. Each of us had our own room on the second floor, complete with a very low bed made of wood, and a bathroom with modern ceramic textures. There was plenty of talking and some laughing as people became immersed in the experience. Personally, I had chosen to stay silent for the full duration.

Well, mostly silent.

As you can imagine, we bumped into each other quite a bit, and I made sure to whisper a quiet apology whenever that happened. My whispers often kicked off a rather amusing exchange. I was the only Thai person taking part in the retreat, which meant I was the only one with a distinct accent other than the guides who maintained the experience. In the apologies that followed any bodily collision, others would pick up on my accent and request services like food and water. So, other than the occasional "sorry" and "no, I don't work here," my silence remained unbroken for the duration of my stay.

After seventy-two hours, I began to perceive what seemed to be the edges of objects around me, which should have been impossible. Strangest of all, they would not vanish when I closed my eyes. In fact, there was no discernable difference between having my eyes open or closed. It seemed as though I was now seeing images through my mind's eye.

In the absence of light, of course, our visual perception is greatly diminished. However, we can perceive some level of visual information, not as a result of external light, but the presence of an internal light. This is a phenomenon called phosphenes. It is the perception of light or colors not caused by external stimuli, but generated within the visual system itself. They can be induced by mechanical, electrical, or magnetic stimulation of the retina or visual cortex.

There is also ongoing research and debate about the role of the pineal gland in visual perception, especially in relation to the production of DMT. While some researchers suggest that DMT may influence our perception of reality and potentially lead to altered states of consciousness or mystical experiences, there is currently no definitive evidence that links the pineal gland's activity to the generation of internal light, or visual perception without external light sources. But, according to my own eyes (well, according to my own *something*) after only the first 72 hours of light deprivation in absolute darkness, without a spec of light to be found, my mind was somehow receiving visual information.

Over the course of the week, those images slowly evolved to become more than simply edges, but visions, like actual movies playing out in my mind. It's difficult to describe, but I could sense the sight entering my mind through a particular spot at the center of my forehead, just above my eyes. This area is what's commonly referred to as the "third eye," and also happens to be the location of the pineal gland. If I was already experiencing this kind of sight within the first few days, I was thrilled by the mystery of what awaited me after as many weeks.

On a more tangible and physical level, my remaining senses were already immensely amplified. We were primarily served fruit for our mealtime, and the flavor seemed completely out of this world. I had eaten papaya all my life, but never tasted anything like whatever heavenly version of it they were bringing us.

There was, of course, nothing truly out of the ordinary about the food, but without vision to dominate my other senses, they were free to thrive and magnify every little experience. I found myself bumping into less people because, even if both of us were silent, we could sense each other's body heat before impact.

Collisions became less common for one other reason— there were less people inhabiting the space. The retreat had a policy in place for people who found something in the darkness that they could not cope with. Anyone could leave at any time, but once they pass through the exit, they cannot return.

By the end of the first week, a significant yet unknown number of people had departed the experience. The darkness of the retreat had amplified whatever darkness they had within them. To be clear, when I say darkness I do not mean "evil". If I thought darkness was a strictly evil thing, then I certainly would not have wrapped it around myself like a blanket.

The darkness inside those who left was, in all likelihood, more of a work-in-progress, or perhaps you could call it a construction site of spirit and mind. Perhaps it was trauma, or a discomfort with stillness, or parts of themselves that they never tried to understand. The fact that they were there and engaging in the experience meant that it was something they were working on, not some evil presence lurking within. Whatever their work-in-progress was, it made the retreat uncomfortable for them and, in the end, intolerable.

Confrontations with these unsettling images, emotions,

or sensory experiences are not mere disruptions, but rather integral parts of the healing process. Often, these emotions and experiences are magnified to facilitate clearing and cleansing.

This process mirrors the experiences of fasting or detoxification. The initial 72 hours typically present the greatest challenge, as both the mind and body undergo a rigorous detoxification process. However, once this initial phase is traversed, individuals begin to enter a phase of restoration and rejuvenation.

The ambience was quieter during the second week, and the effects of the darkness on my mind began to intensify. I had signed up for acupuncture and, as you might imagine, having a couple of dozen needles penetrating my skin while I had a heightened sense of touch was immensely painful. I knew this going into it but, the same as the rest of the retreat, I wanted to experience the intensity. Even more, I wanted to feel the enhanced version of the after effects, and they did not disappoint.

WOW.

The outcome was one of tremendous relief and relaxation, and a sense of cohesive energy flowed all throughout my body. It was another prominent example of how pain can be a doorway to pleasure, darkness to enlightenment.

Soon, time began to contort; my behavior shifted from external to internal. During the first week, I had participated in group meditation and engaged in group activities like Tai chi, qigong, meditation, and Taoist yoga.

However, starting from the eighth day, I felt the need for more quietness and stillness to process my inner experience. I knew I could do this best without worrying about schedules or specific activities. Instead, I simply allowed myself to *be*. I meditated silently for extended lengths of time, communicating with my inner visual and auditory messages, observing sensory experiences, and recording my findings in the dark.

Or, more accurately, I *tried* to record them. As it turns out, muscle-memory alone is not enough to bring the ability to write into an abyss. I had no way of knowing this at the time, but I was really just jotting down organized scribbles. At least I would be leaving the retreat with something you could call modern art.

As my sense of time drifted further from my conscious mind, I found my appetite begin to decline, and thus began my final fourteen days, which I lived without solid food, relying only on fresh juice and water to keep my physical body functioning.

Although I had found the group meditation, yoga, and tai chi to be beneficial, I wanted to fully experience being within myself. Fortunately, although I truly love to socialize, it has never been an activity that I need to be happy. So, I spent more time alone in my room, keeping up with physical activity by way of gentle stretching and moving throughout my space.

Eventually, even that limited physical activity fell away from me. I would like to say that this was a strong choice of potent will-power out of dedication to inward discovery. But, dear reader, I will be honest with you.

I was feeling monumentally lazy.

This lethargic state was limited to my body, however. My mind was heading in the opposite direction. I experimented with mental exercise, practicing Tai Chi in my mind every day. It was a practice I was familiar with from guiding others at my wellness center who were physically unable to move. This approach allowed them to experience the psychological benefits of exercise that were otherwise unavailable to them.

Physical activity was bumped even further down my list of priorities because the alternative was so enticing. Off and on, my mind would treat me to what some might call world-class entertainment.

I have never been too interested in movies and television, and when I do watch them I am careful about what I expose myself to. What we consume can have a powerful impact on our minds, thoughts, actions, and overall well-being, both emotional and physical.

In this case, instead of a digital screen, it was my mind that was connecting me with what I can only call "movies". I saw past and future events, memories I had long-since known of, and others which had been buried deep within my mind.

One moment, I would be lying on my ground in quiet contemplation, the next I would find myself walking through a forest, or back in Lumphini Park, where I had seen tai chi practitioners for the first time.

The ability to distinguish between visions of the past and future hinged on various factors. Past events often presented themselves as scenes from different eras, distinguished by attire, hairstyles, and manners that reflect specific periods in history.

On the other hand, visions of the future often presented me with an older version of myself, with age evidently etched onto my features. Future events were further inferred from futuristic environments, characterized by modern architectural designs and airborne vehicles. These visions could arise from the realm of imagination, or from my mind's grappling with duality while existing in a non-linear time-space continuum.

In such a state, the concepts of past and future dissolve, leaving only the present moment. It is within this present moment that we 'recall' the past and 'envision' the future, though these perceptions may not necessarily align with our usual understanding of time.

All throughout the second week, I found myself constantly watching these internal movies, which I believe focused on self-exploration, personal identity, and our connections with others. They encompassed various aspects of the self, including perceptions, feelings, and emotions.

These movies were not limited to visual images; they also featured sounds that my mind could only ever imagine in silence, as well as a sense of smell, tactile vibrations, temperatures. All of these sensations were dialed-up and interconnected with one another.

At times, these visions appeared as symbols, shapes, or colors. Other times, they manifested as faces—both pleasant and unpleasant, with some being downright disturbing.

Somewhere around the third week, time ceased to matter as I transcended its constraints. Perhaps that is a difficult thing to imagine, but it's best explained like this: Imagine walking along the surface of a vast, frozen river. Suddenly, you fall through the surface and into the rushing current below. You're disoriented, and moving with the invisible force of a current.

For me, that river was time itself. I was still traveling along the same bends and heading downstream, but I was unable to see the river bank to mark my location. Instead, I was freely flowing, naturally guided forward with seemingly no agency of my own.

Within the latter half of the retreat, I was treated to a truly profound encounter. Near-death experiences all follow similar patterns. When some people die and then return, they say they feel as though they became a star, or part of the Sun, or simply one with everything. Some report going to a place of pure joy, or a more mystical one inhabited by the souls of others.

I was able to fall into that pattern without actually coming close to death. Or rather, I'm fairly certain I wasn't near death. It started when I felt my consciousness, or soul, exiting my body. It was a fast and disorienting feeling of not simply floating out of my physical self, but spinning out of it and being flung into the cosmos. I became a star among other stars, I felt beautiful and unconditional love. I had gone to a place beyond description, one that no human language could ever possibly capture. I couldn't guess how long I had been there before—

VOOP.

I was pulled back into my body. It was the most distinct transition out of a vision that I had experienced. Whereas my mental movies would come and go, this time felt like a quick visit to another place, a glimpse at existence there, and then a deliberate return home.

Although visions continued for the rest of my stay, I was never able to return to that place. In a way, it made my visit all-the-more special, as if I had been allowed a glimpse of a forbidden space. Instead of longing to return, I still think of my time in the stars as a gift, one that I could only unwrap once.

Then, seemingly out of nowhere, the teachers announced that it was time to prepare to exit. Time had moved remarkably fast, to the point where I could hardly believe I would be reemerging into a world of vision in less than a day.

Gathering with the others in the hall, I couldn't help noticing how much quieter the group had become. In part, I knew this was caused by the others slipping into a calmer and more introspective state. It was also likely that we had lost a good number of people; I wondered how many had decided to leave the retreat early.

We were reminded that, although we would be departing deep in the night, our environment would seem intensely bright. Our pupils had dilated so much that even the ambient light provided by the stars would hurt our eyes.

Each of us was handed a pair of cardboard, disposable sunglasses. They were similar in design to the half-red half-blue glasses you would wear for an old 3D movie, except they were tinted instead of colored. This meant that, for just that one evening, I had in my possession something that is coveted by fashionistas and rock stars alike—an excuse to wear sunglasses at night.

To avoid confusion, we held hands and guided each other in a single file line through a series of doors, and soon stepped out into what could only be called a bright night. Although there was no moon, and the only light sources were the stars, the glow was indeed too intense for the naked eye.

As I took in my environment, my eyes fell not only on the foliage, but the people around me. I was shocked to discover that out of the forty participants who had entered the darkness with me, only ten remained. That meant seventy-five percent of those in attendance had come up against something they were not ready to face. I don't look at this as a failure on their part. Rather, it was a touch of over-ambition, something that they might choose to dial back and take in a different direction along their personal journeys.

Wearing shades to temper the night's vibrancy, we were all guided out into a beautiful garden of trees, bamboo, and flowers, all of which were silhouetted by the spectacular cosmos. In addition to the stars above, I noticed an orange glow down the trail ahead of me. It was coming from a bed of hot coals that had been laid out to receive us. Once there, we would have a brief ceremony to celebrate our return before walking barefoot across the scorching heat.

Walking across red-hot coals is a spiritual practice found in various indigenous cultures and in certain mind-training traditions. In some cultures, fire-walking is a rite of passage, a test of courage, or a means to overcome fear. It is believed that successfully completing the walk demonstrates mental and emotional strength, as well as spiritual fortitude. Participants often prepare for the ritual through prayer, meditation, or other spiritual practices that help them achieve a trance-like state, which enables them to walk over the hot coals without experiencing pain or injury.

Our preparation, in many ways, had been three weeks long. The final ceremony before the walk was simply a sendoff. We celebrated together and listened to the master speak one last time.

Truly, the act we were about to perform was a demonstration of the power of mind over body. It serves as a way to prove that with the proper mental focus and control, one can overcome physical limitations and pain. The practice builds self-confidence, discipline, and mastery over the mind. Now, it was our turn to try.

The master went first, further driving home our trust and fully-committed belief that no harm would come to us. He reached the other side, turned, and smiled at us. Then he showed us his feet—no signs of burn.

Suddenly, anyone in the group who had been nervous was now excited to try. I was a few people back in the line. Looking down at the walk, the glow was so brilliant that the coals appeared to be holding back a subterranean star. Even though I had recently experienced floating among a field of stars, the prospect of walking across the surface of one with my actual, physical body was still a concerning premise.

Regardless of what I had been through, I still felt a natural aversion to what my mind perceived as potential bodily injury, but my mind was in such a unique state that the aversion was unable to evolve into fear. Soon, it was gone altogether. I hadn't conjured up intense bravery or beaten back fear, because suddenly there was nothing to fear. There was no need to be brave. There was simply *doing.*

I watched as one participant after another completed their walk, fearless and with no sign of pain. When my turn came, I looked across the 12-foot stretch of incredible heat and knew with certainty that I would complete the walk unharmed. Upon taking my first step, my nervous system reported warmth to my mind, but no pain.

Eventually, my feet reached the cool grass on the other side of the walk. I waited and watched the others perform the same ritual, each of them remaining stoic and unharmed until they reached the other side, at which point they would let their enthusiasm and pride show.

We said our farewells, thanked our master, and headed to the private cabins that had been provided for the final night of the retreat. Mine was a small, wooden structure situated within what seemed to be nature's finest. I felt so alive, so active, that I thought I would have trouble sleeping. Instead, I landed in bed and shut down completely.

The next morning, I felt reborn. The cabin had a back porch that overlooked a small, private garden and a beautiful tropical forest. My eyes, instead of being irritated by the light, simply took in the environment in unreal, indescribably vibrance. Can you imagine what the first sunrise was like? It was like nothing I had ever seen before. On top of that, all of my other senses were still in an amplified state. Every touch was magnified, every sound was in high fidelity.

Instead of rushing to reconnect with my life, I couldn't seem to fathom what might even exist beyond the view from that porch. I simply relaxed there, drinking juice while watching, listening, and feeling my surroundings. Some of my observations morphed into questions. Instead of simply appreciating everything I saw, I asked myself: How was it even possible that the world was so beautiful?

I did my best to etch the answer into my mind. The world is beautiful in many different ways, but only if we know how to perceive that beauty. The good news is that in order to gain that perception, one doesn't need to commit to three weeks in total darkness. The key to this perception is simple curiosity. If you are seeking beauty, you can rest assured that it is also seeking you.

If reading about my experience in darkness has inspired you to try the same, I'm happy to report that the trend of darkness retreats has only grown with time. Some offer shorter experiences, others are longer. I can only encourage you to pursue your interest—with a caveat.

Do the work first.

This is not something that you are meant to conquer or enter with the mindset of satisfying a dare. It's worth noting that "work" in this context is one of the most pleasant and fulfilling things you can do. Yoga, meditation, therapy, tai chi, contemplation—all of these things are "work," but in many ways they carry the benefits of a nice, warm bath.

The darkness retreat gave me many things, including spectacular visions, unique perspective, an appreciation and openness to beauty, but there is one gift that I didn't fully unwrap until leaving my cabin for the last time. It's a belief that, two decades later, I still carry with me. As I left the retreat behind, I thought with certainty, beyond the shadow of doubt:

I am fearless.

The Killing Fields

During my college years, I engaged in numerous volunteer activities, always approaching life with a beginner's mind, curious and open to exploring new opportunities. College, for me, was not just an academic endeavor but a playground of possibilities where I could mold my passion and drive into tangible experiences.

One opportunity that particularly intrigued me arose during a seminar on global humanitarian efforts. As I learned about the plight of refugees in Southeast Asia, particularly along the border of Thailand and Cambodia, I knew that I wanted to contribute in some way. I wanted to take my volunteering experience to a more impactful level.

Among the refugee camps that caught my attention were Kao I Dang and Site 2, located near the Thai-Cambodian borders. The situation in these camps was dire, with thousands of displaced Cambodians seeking refuge from the horrors they had experienced in their homeland. The term "The Killing Fields" often echoed in our briefings, and the chilling significance of those words was something that required deeper understanding.

"The Killing Fields" is a term associated with the Cambodian Genocide, a haunting and tragic reminder of human cruelty. During the late 1970s, under the Khmer Rouge regime, areas known as killing fields were designated for mass executions and atrocities on a horrific scale. Following the Cambodian Civil War, the Khmer Rouge sought to establish an agrarian utopia, forcing urban populations into the countryside and subjecting the Cambodian people to unimaginable brutality.

As the violence escalated, many Cambodians sought refuge across the border in Thailand. These refugee camps, like the ones I volunteered in, became a lifeline, providing a safe haven for individuals, families, and children who had lost everything.

After graduation, I was fortunate enough to be offered a position as a health education supervisor in these very camps. My responsibilities would be manifold: training the medics, refugees who underwent a short course in basic medicine, first aid, and self-care; overseeing the malnourished children's ward, housing an average of about 200 children at any given time; and even managing communication via walkie-talkies, a responsibility that felt both thrilling and significant—at the time this technology was more associated with soldiers and spies.

The landscape of the camp, though stark and devoid of trees, bore a certain beauty. It was a place where life had to be reconstructed with the limited resources at hand—red dirt, bamboo structures, and the necessary supplies like food, water, and medicine, all carefully arranged to accommodate the immense population of over 150,000 refugees. Witnessing this environment firsthand, I was struck by its profound effect on the human psyche, and by the realization that, although temporary, it had become a real and significant home for so many.

As I walked through the camp, interacting with its residents and becoming part of their daily lives, I couldn't help but feel a deep sense of admiration and compassion. The individuals who had turned this barren landscape into a place of belonging, community, and resilience were living testimonies to the strength of the human spirit. Their ability to create a sense of home in such adverse conditions, their laughter amidst hardship, their determination to not just survive but thrive, was a testament to an innate longing for hope and a brighter future.

As I started my work in the refugee camp on the Thai/ Cambodia border in the mid-1980s, I quickly realized that my college education had only skimmed the surface of the reality I was about to face. It was an immersion into a world marked by loss, terror, resilience, and human strength.

The gravity of the situation became more apparent with each new arrival at the camp. Many of the refugees who arrived had harrowing tales of survival, recounting the horrors they witnessed in the killing fields. Men, women, and children alike would share their stories, often through tears and broken words, speaking of family members lost, dreams shattered, and homes destroyed. The stories they shared were fresh wounds, heart-wrenching and raw, serving as a stark reminder of the cruelty and inhumanity that had plagued Cambodia during that dark period.

In the camp, the faces of loss were everywhere. I encountered individuals who had seen their entire families wiped out by the Khmer Rouge's atrocities. Mothers who had lost children, children who had lost parents, and elders who had lost everyone they once knew. Some had escaped only by sheer luck or by hiding in the dense jungles for days, evading capture and death.

One young girl I worked with had lost both parents and had been on the run for weeks before finding safety in the camp. Her eyes, still filled with terror, would often look around as if expecting danger at any moment. Building trust with her and many others like her required patience, empathy, and a genuine commitment to understanding their pain.

One of the most challenging aspects of my role was providing support and counseling to survivors grappling with severe trauma and post-traumatic stress disorder, or PTSD. It was not merely about administering medication or conducting health screenings. It was about engaging with deep, emotional scars that had profoundly affected their lives. It was heartbreaking to witness their pain, to see adults and children alike trapped in memories they couldn't escape. This was my first brush with a malady that, all these years later, we are on the verge of near-miraculous treatments thanks to medical use of psychedelics.

In the midst of the camp's despair, there were moments of profound reward and connection. Seeing how a safe and caring environment in the camp, along with access to basic necessities and medical care, could spark the beginning of healing was deeply satisfying. A smile returning to a child's face, a sense of community developing among the refugees, the sharing of stories and cultural traditions - these were signs of life re-emerging from the shadow of death.

Despite the adversity they had faced, the resilience of the refugees was truly inspiring. There was a sense of solidarity, an unspoken understanding that they were survivors, not victims, and that they were determined to rebuild their lives and maintain a sense of hope for the future.

The camp was a melting pot of cultures, languages, and traditions. Though stark in appearance, it blossomed into a vibrant community where people from various ethnic backgrounds came together. What had initially seemed like an ocean of red dirt and makeshift bamboo structures transformed into a place where human connections transcended the barriers of nationality and language. Bonds were forged in shared experience, and a sense of unity emerged among those who had suffered the brutal effects of war and displacement.

Efforts were made to provide necessary education and vocational training for adults, empowering them to acquire skills that would be valuable for their future. Makeshift classrooms were established, and I watched as refugees embraced opportunities to learn, to create, and to build new paths for themselves. Whether they would eventually return to Cambodia or relocate to other countries for resettlement, the seeds of transformation were being sown. Analyzing, cultivating, and spreading these seeds—whatever form they may take—would one day become my life's work

As international organization workers, we were not allowed to stay at camp sites due to safety concerns. Our residence was in the town of Arunyaprathet, the closest town on the Thai side near the Thailand-Cambodia border. We were part of the medical team at COERR (Catholic Office of Emergency Relief for Refugees), and our main base was Site 2, the refugee camp where we provided essential medical services.

Every morning, the medical team embarked on our journey from Arunyaprathet to Site 2. Traveling in a caravan of 2-3 vans, the 6-mile drive could take up to 2 hours due to the rough dirt roads and the need to avoid areas that might be susceptible to bombings or hidden dangers. Safety was of paramount importance, and we were vigilant to ensure our well-being during the journey.

We departed at 7 am sharp and reached the camp by 9 am. Upon arrival, our first task was to unload the necessary medical supplies and set up the pharmacies and clinic for the day's operations. With specific responsibilities assigned, we received a briefing on the day's plan and objectives. The clinic would soon become bustling with activity as we attended to a steady flow of outpatients, treating various ailments and injuries.

Since not everyone had access to a walkie-talkie, it was crucial for team members to stay in close proximity during their routine work. Our dedication to providing medical care to the refugees drove us to be readily available and accessible throughout the day.

I grew accustomed to the excitement and unpredictability that each day brought, and "expect the unexpected" had become both my mantra and guiding principle.

As Code Name Sierra One, I held a weighty responsibility despite my petite stature of five feet four inches and approximately one hundred pounds. As the second-in-command for my team's security, I worked diligently with COERR, which had been assigned the code name "Sierra." In those days, well before the advent of smartphones, our team relied on three walkie talkies for distance communication.

Ben, a half English-Thai, bore the code name Sierra Zero and was in charge of our COERR team's security. The Thai Military operated under the code name Tango, with the Tango team responsible for overall security.

Whenever Tango detected any suspicious activities, such as shelling, bombings, explosions, or gunshots nearby, they promptly reached out to each team, including us international workers. This ensured that we stayed informed and aware of the prevailing situations.

The security situation at the camp was classified into four levels, each indicating the degree of urgency and potential danger. Situation 1 implied that there were some incidents occurring further away from the camp, prompting us to exercise caution. We encountered Situation 1 frequently, almost on a daily basis.

In Situation 2, unsafe incidents drew near, necessitating us to be prepared to secure all our equipment, including mobile pharmacies and vehicles, that we brought to the camp to provide services. This preparation was essential in case we needed to quickly evacuate the camp when the situation escalated to level 3.

If that moment came it was critical that we act swiftly. We gathered all our belongings, coordinated with every team member, and left the camp to seek safer ground. In these instances, the safety and well-being of everyone took precedence.

Situation 4 was the most severe level, indicating an imminent threat to our lives. In such dire circumstances, we did whatever was necessary to find shelter or, if possible, reach a nearby safe area such as a bunker. Situation 4 signified grave danger, such as a bombing or a direct attack on the camp.

Over the two years of my commissioned work there, I encountered Situation 4 only twice. Fortunately, on both occasions, we managed to stay safe. The ability to swiftly respond to each situation and the teamwork among us were instrumental in ensuring our well-being during these critical moments.

By 2 pm each day, we packed up and prepared to leave the campsite, returning to our residence in Arunyaprathet. The long and eventful day came to a close, leaving us with a mix of emotions—from concern for the refugees, who faced fear each night in the campsite, to a sense of fulfillment in being able to make a difference in the lives of those who sought our care and compassion.

I had the opportunity to interact with colleagues from various international organizations and NGOs who were involved in the camp's operation. The collaboration and coordination among these organizations were crucial in ensuring the efficient delivery of aid and support to the refugees. It was heartening to witness individuals from different backgrounds and nationalities come together for a common cause, putting aside any differences in the pursuit of humanitarian goals.

We were all united by a shared mission, and the connections I formed with my colleagues were rich and rewarding. Together, we navigated challenges, celebrated successes, and supported one another through the emotional highs and lows of our work.

The rich culture of the camp was a vibrant source of life and energy. The refugees, hailing from diverse backgrounds, used creativity and innovation to recreate the fabric of their homelands in this temporary shelter. They would often gather together to sing traditional songs, perform dances, and narrate stories that gave them a sense of belonging and connection to their roots.

Despite the challenges of living in bamboo shelters with dirt floors and the ever-present uncertainty about the future, the people found ways to create pockets of joy. The vibrancy of their festivals, the aroma of traditional meals, and the colors of their artistic expressions offered a unique window into their world, preserving the dignity and richness of their culture amid the challenging conditions.

My days were filled with the innocence and smiles of the young. In the children's ward, I was entrusted with the care of around 200 young souls, their bodies often tragically weakened by malnutrition.

I recall the ingenuity with which we treated a ten-year-old girl with a fractured leg, using a recycled IV saline bottle for traction and a wooden branch as the weight to stabilize her leg. This instance was emblematic of our resourcefulness, using what little we had to bring healing and comfort.

The smiles of these children, playing with toys crafted from recycled materials—a doll from old cloth, a toy car from weathered wood—were symbols of hope and joy. They revealed the remarkable adaptability and creativity that could be found even in the direst of situations.

The process of recovery for many of these children was a testament to the transformative power of humanitarian aid. Their smiles grew wider, their bodies stronger, and their laughter louder with each passing day.

Life in the camp remained a daily challenge, an endless cycle of making do with limited resources and overcrowded conditions. Amid the hustle and bustle of new arrivals and the continuous struggle for survival, the camp's dynamics were ever-changing.

Water, rice, and beans became the lifelines of the camp. Every Wednesday, when the water truck rumbled into view, a palpable sense of relief washed over the camp. Lines would quickly form, each person clutching their empty containers, waiting patiently to fill up their large 3 and 5-gallon jugs. This water would sustain them through the week, quenching thirst and aiding in daily tasks.

Alongside these basic provisions, some families found small pockets of joy in cultivating vegetables around their bamboo huts. The homegrown produce added a touch of familiarity to their otherwise Spartan meals.

Within the bamboo walls of the camp's medical facility lay a world of pain and healing, suffering and recovery. The wards were simple structures with low bamboo beds set on red dirt, covered only by large open-air shelters.

As part of the medical team, I was responsible for tending to the various wards, including the adult, women's, children's, and the TB Tuberculosis wards. Every patient, regardless of age or ailment, received our full care and attention.

The women and mother ward was a place of life's most profound transitions. I witnessed the incredible strength of mothers giving birth on hard bamboo beds, following traditional methods of healing that had been passed down through generations.

Among the adult males, I saw the ravages of malaria and the scars of gunshot wounds—the legacies of nocturnal fighting in the jungle, leaving behind physical and emotional wounds that were hard to heal.

Even though the camp was meant for civilians, we found ourselves attending to military personnel, their amputated limbs, and shattered bodies. Those scenes were both tragic and heart-wrenching, a stark testament to the cruel realities of war.

Some mornings were particularly haunting, with men arriving, holding their amputated limbs, soaked in blood, and pleading for help. Things of this nature would occur on the same day as striking symbols of vitality, like assisting a twin birth inside a moving ambulance, on our way to Kao I Dang, the surgery base camp operated by the International Red Cross.

The camp was indeed a place of paradoxes, where immense suffering coexisted with immense resilience.

Then, there was my time outside the camp, which was not solely for rest and recovery. Driven by an insatiable curiosity, I found myself drawn to explore the unique culture and traditions of the Cambodian people and the nearby refugee camp sites like Site 8 or Panat Nikon.

The culture seemed to me like a time capsule, with much of the music and traditions harkening back to the 1960s, despite being in the 1980s. The limited resources might have restricted access to more contemporary items, but this didn't dampen their spirit.

One of the most rewarding aspects of my exploration was delving into the traditional healing practices of the Cambodian people. This journey brought me face-to-face with local shamans, mystical figures who bridged the gap between the physical world and the spiritual realm. Their rituals, dances, and chants were mesmerizing, providing a fascinating glimpse into a belief system that was both deeply spiritual and intrinsically connected to the well-being of the community.

The Cambodian indigenous healing practices were not confined to physical health alone. They embraced a holistic view of well-being, aligning the mind, body, and spirit. It was a privilege to witness local healers skillfully preparing and administering herbal remedies with reverence and care.

These practices transcended mere medicinal applications. Cambodian shamanic healers, regarded as spiritual intermediaries, played an essential role in their traditions. Their connection with the spirit world enabled them to facilitate healing through rituals and ceremonies, guided by a belief system that may not have been fully understood but was profoundly respected.

My experiences with the UNHCR, both inside and outside the camp, had a profound impact on my understanding of "war." As a young girl, war seemed synonymous with conflict, trauma, and human suffering. But as the years unfolded and my perspective matured, I began to perceive war in a more nuanced light.

I came to see it not merely as a physical event but as a complex reflection of human evolution and consciousness. It appeared to me as a cyclical pattern within humanity, alternating between destructive tendencies and creative possibilities.

This realization led me to appreciate that the path to lasting peace lay not just in addressing the external signs of conflict but in nurturing our internal landscape. By tapping into our innate intelligence, practicing mindfulness, and developing a deep awareness of our thoughts and emotions, we can break free from the patterns that perpetuate war and suffering.

This understanding of war transformed it from a distressing reality into a call for personal transformation. It became an invitation to recognize our spiritual essence and choose a life free from internal conflicts. By embracing peace, love, joy, and fulfillment within ourselves, we become agents of change in the world.

Each individual's commitment to inner peace contributes to our collective well-being. By shifting our consciousness towards harmony, compassion, and understanding, we move humanity away from the cycle of war and towards a world where an enlightened society prevails.

As I left the camp for the last time, I knew that it would forever remain a part of me. The red dirt, the bamboo shelters, the faces of those I had come to know – they were all part of a story that had changed me. A story of survival, of hope, of human connection. A story that continues to inspire my journey and my belief in the endless capacity of the human heart.

In the decades of my life's journey that have passed since then, I have grown immensely. Today, I stand as a mature and empathetic doctor and guide, with wisdom and compassion that only time and experience can bestow. I have come to recognize the profound impact one person can have, and I am more determined than ever to use my skills and insights for the betterment of society and the well-being of those around me.

I know that the sights seem disturbing, the experience

psychologically scarring, but the way my mind has chosen to process these memories has been kind to me. My amygdala shielded me from holding on to emotional trauma, while allowing me to absorb the moments of joy. This has kept me in a perpetual state of exploration, approaching life with the enthusiasm of both a student and a teacher.

I stand ready to teach others about life, to reignite hope, rekindle love, and empower people to live fully. I believe that we are meant to do something greater than ourselves, and we can be conduits of healing. As human beings, we possess the capacity to embrace life with all its beauty and challenges, guided by compassion and empathy.

The memories of the refugee camp and the lessons I learned continue to shape my purpose, fueling my desire to be of service, to touch lives, and to work towards a more just and compassionate world. With a heart filled with gratitude, I move forward, ready to inspire others and embrace the endless possibilities that life offers.

I carry with me the profound understanding that the pursuit of humanitarian work knows no boundaries. It can transcend any barriers that may divide us, and it is a universal calling that unites us in the shared endeavor to alleviate suffering and bring healing. In reflecting on this transformative chapter, I am filled with gratitude and a deep sense of purpose, ready to continue the journey and embrace the challenges and opportunities that lie ahead.

The Dead Mentor

I can't be sure of exactly when Ted died, but I do know the time we were supposed to meet on that day. We had an 11 AM appointment on September 14th, 2004 at my wellness center on the day that he disappeared. Meetings like this one were a weekly engagement for us, where I guided him through meditation and various Tai Chi movements. So far, he had not missed one without calling, but I had been so wrapped up in what was proving to be a busy day that I didn't think to follow up with a phone call when he failed to appear.

The next day, I was on the receiving end of a call, but it wasn't from Ted. The FBI had looked at his calendar and seen that I was on his schedule for the day, and indeed close to the time, that he had vanished without a trace. I had very little information to offer the agent on the other end of the line—only that Ted was typically good about keeping appointments, except for this one. The fact that his disappearance had already escalated to an FBI investigation told me that I wasn't the only part of his schedule he had broken that day. I hung up feeling deep concern for my mentor and friend.

I had met Ted several years prior, when my business endeavors in Greenville, South Carolina were still gaining steam. At that time, every business endeavor in the area was also a work-in-progress. In the years before I met Ted, Greenville had been of "Goldilocks" size—small enough for entrepreneurs to know each other and work to help each other, yet large enough for sizable investments of money, time, and effort to be available.

I became very active as a volunteer in the community, helping to put on networking events. In a way, I was already becoming somewhat of a poster child for The American Dream, having moved here from a foreign country and found success. It seemed as though I had business meetings or networking events every morning. I took part in larger gatherings that were attended by bankers, brokers, and local government officials, including the mayor himself.

It was an ever-expanding group of leaders and influential people who truly wanted to help create a successful community, and it was through this vast network that I eventually met Ted. He was known for his successful business endeavors, persona of kindness. He was the retired president of a multinational company whose products you may have in your home currently. Since his retirement, instead of retreating to permanent residence on a yacht, Ted became an extremely active philanthropist and investor. As he was leaving the business world behind, he was doing everything in his power to mentor the next generation of entrepreneurs. His work took him far beyond the confines of for-profit business. He was incredibly active in charity events, and for that, he was well known and respected in the community.

Ted's life first overlapped with mine at a networking event in the Greenville Chamber of Commerce. His ever-smiling face resonated deeply with me. We clicked instantly, although this might be less a product of our compatibility and more a result of Ted's open and friendly nature.

Given this alignment, I was quick to ask Ted to mentor me. He graciously accepted. The relationship wasn't anything as official as a business coach. In terms of business ventures in Greenville, a mentor was simply someone who connected you to other people with mutual interests or complimenting abilities. I couldn't have been more thrilled, especially considering all of the successful people Ted had mentored in the past.

I believe this was one of the many keys to Ted's own success. It wasn't simply an ability to negotiate, smile, pitch ideas, or make smart investments. He was emotionally invested in making a positive impact on the community. Even beyond that, his secret ingredient was relationships, and sharing those connections with others only made him more valuable to those around him, myself included. Over the years, Ted connected me with financiers and even some high-ranking government officials. If I found myself at a dinner party and sitting across the table from the U.S. Ambassador to Thailand, it was likely because of Ted. Meetings like those are what enabled me to pursue many of my current dreams and aspirations.

All of this is to say: Ted was like a father to me.

Flashing forward from there to the moments after my call with the FBI, I felt compelled to help, but equally unable to do so. Fortunately, I knew someone who just might be able to.

Charlotte was experienced in a skill known as "psychic remote viewing", skilled enough that it was actually her primary function within the CIA. At the time, I knew very little about the practice other than its basic process and incredible potential. I called Charlotte that night, and gave her as few details about the situation as possible. My limited knowledge on remote viewing already included that minimizing upfront details was an important part of remote viewing. Going into the process with too much detail could taint the viewing with preconceived notions and imagery, resulting in a less trustworthy report.

So, I gave her the barebones of the situation and my intentions. I was seeking details about my missing mentor, and that was all. Charlotte was happy to help, as she always was, but warned me that I might not want to put much trust in her findings. She had already done quite a bit of this work that very day, and adding a last-minute viewing into her already packed schedule would be difficult. Information derived from her tired state of mind was likely to be inaccurate.

Still, she was a good friend, and she promised to do her best. On my end, all I could do was meditate and wait. That night, I had a harder time falling asleep than usual.

I'm saying this as someone who has worked diligently to hone the skill of stilling their mind. Suffice it to say: Ted's disappearance had knocked me off-kilter.

The next day, Charlotte sent me a report, detailing everything she had found. It was three pages long and written directly into the body of an email, in what I soon learned to be standard remote viewing language, using narratives, coordinates, numbers, shapes, and energetic properties for description.

The summation of the report was a concerning one. Charlotte had perceived a young couple, large male and small female, and a third entity she couldn't quite grasp details on, in addition to Ted himself. That was straightforward information, but the other details were even more upsetting—a pointed gun, white rope, and chest pain. It was impossible to tell if this was from being hit with something, or shot with the aforementioned gun. Lastly, she saw a lonely and abandoned structure in a rural area. In her conclusion, Charlotte did her best to emotionally prepare me with a warning. It was likely that my mentor was already dead.

I was taken aback by the report, and found myself at a loss for what to do next. I didn't want to contact Ted's family. They were already dealing with unimaginable stress, and I didn't want to pile on top of that any frightening information that may or may not even be true.

Another alternative was to contact the FBI to tip them off, but just a few seconds of thinking revealed to me that it wasn't actually an option. A tip like that would do one of two things. It could be patently false and unhelpful, or suspiciously accurate, therefore implicating me in a crime that had already been committed.

My concern went beyond criminal implications; there were cultural conflicts to consider. I was in an area deep within the Bible Belt of the United States. If you picture the year 2004, my act of merely introducing concepts like meditation and yoga was audacious enough. What if I were to bring in information from a remote viewing? Who would believe me if I said the details had been derived from a non-ordinary state of consciousness? I didn't want to imagine the challenge of explaining a psychic information source to the conventional mindset that was prevalent at that time and place. So, guided by a mindful perspective, I chose to maintain stillness and wait for events to naturally unfold.

Within 72 hours, the discovery of Ted's body made national news. Between what was publicly disclosed and the details I later learned from his wife, the connection to Charlotte's viewing were clear. Ted had been restrained with a white rope, the chest pain Charlotte had perceived was the heart attack that Ted suffered while he was in captivity, and his body was discovered buried beneath an abandoned barn.

The details Charlotte had sent were more vast and accurate than perhaps either of us had expected. Right in my email inbox, I had evidence of a non-conventional channel for investigation. At the time she compiled her findings, no one, not Ted's family, the investigators, or myself, had any way of knowing what Charlotte had perceived.

I wasn't able to verify the other connections between reality and Charlotte's viewing until information was released about the perpetrators, a man and a woman who had brought their baby with them for the abduction. This must have been the third entity that Charlotte had picked up on. Apparently, the couple had intended to hold him for ransom, but his heart attack brought their scheme crashing down, and ultimately cost the world one extraordinary person.

Ted was someone who, when I think of him, I see a mind that is ablaze with creativity. I was so fortunate to have his mentorship to ignite my own success. He had been the glue of his community, and the positivity he put into his environment only inspired me to try and create a similar, positive impact on the world. I had always wanted to find, and help others find, the joy in life. Ted was one who helped me learn how to not simply find that joy, but *create* it.

However, life and the joy within it are complicated things. With his loss confirmed, my mind instantly took me back to a strange conversation we had. During one of my last meditation sessions with Ted, he had turned pale and confided something in me that I could barely believe.

"I'm ready to die," he had said.

I couldn't fathom why he would feel that way. He was clearly happy, wealthy, and loved. Why would anyone want a life like that to end? As it turned out, he had been diagnosed with a rare disease. Although he didn't disclose its exact name or nature, he made it clear that his quality of life was on the precipice of a decline. Whatever image Ted had of his future, it was not one he wanted to experience.

I believe that the resurfacing of this memory was my mind trying to comfort me. We might not have been ready to lose Ted but, hopefully, he had been prepared for his own departure. Nothing could ever make Ted's murder a "good" thing, but this idea seemed to make his unnatural death seem more natural when observed from a broader scheme. I recognize that this perhaps my own shallow coping mechanism—we all grieve in unique ways—but it gave me a silver lining of meaning amidst a cloud of chaos. Maybe I could never truly answer the "why" of Ted's death. Some questions have no answers, but there were questions adjacent to these events that I knew I could learn from.

Why and how was Charlotte able to tap into the information in her report?

Could remote viewing show me more about life after death?

The prospect of remote viewing was so fascinating, and so interconnected with many of my other interests, I was compelled to look further into it.

Remote Viewing

My previous knowledge of extrasensory perception in the form of remote viewing had primarily come from conversations with Charlotte. The events surrounding Ted's murder were the first time I encountered a life-altering event that sufficiently piqued my curiosity to explore these phenomena. This fascination with the metaphysical led me to delve head-first into the mysteries of the hidden parts of reality that few people ever get to touch.

Though I had practiced deep meditation and was able to enter non-ordinary or psychedelic states of consciousness, these states of mind did not adhere to the precise protocols of remote viewing, as I was about to learn.

I was very fortunate to be in a position where I didn't need to worry about staying still and making a living. My time in Greenville with Ted and others like him had been fruitful enough that I was free to pursue my interests, and after that week, my interests were 100% driven toward remote viewing.

Charlotte supported my curiosity and offered to connect me with some of her own mentors in the field. I felt as though I was standing on the edge of an enormous lake of knowledge - a lake the size of the cosmos - able to swim in any direction. The opportunity was overwhelming in the best sense of the word. Charlotte helped me choose a path, which brought me to a man named David Morehouse, PhD.

Dr. Morehouse was a former Army officer who had been involved in remote viewing operations and experiments conducted by U.S. Army intelligence and the Stanford Research Institute, where he worked as a "psychic spy" in the late 80s. This was essentially the job that Charlotte was currently performing for the CIA, although it had been significantly more experimental back in David's day.

"Psychic spy" is a title that not many have heard of because, before being discontinued, it was quite the fringe branch of the intelligence community. The project went by different names, including Grill Flame and Stargate. Its primary focus was to evaluate whether individuals could gain and describe information about targets that were blocked from ordinary perception by distance, physical barriers, or even time.

Grill Flame had been founded in the 1970s and, as you can imagine, the U.S. Military and intelligence community were quite keen to see if this was a viable technique for glimpsing into state and strategic secrets of foreign adversaries. The project was based in Fort Meade, Maryland, and operated under the auspices of the Defense Intelligence Agency (DIA) and the Stanford Research

Institute.

Since this book is more focused on rewiring sentience and not winning cold wars, I won't be delving much deeper into the rise and fall of Grill Flame and the Stargate Project. There is plenty of literature available on those programs, some of it written by David himself.

He had previously written a book on his experiences, called "Psychic Warrior: Inside the CIA's Stargate Program." David had encountered a training accident in 1987 which altered his perception and led him to develop psychic abilities. That was when he was recruited into Grill Flame, where he trained his newfound abilities for military intelligence purposes.

Now, although the official government programs and training had come to an end, David continued to share his knowledge with any interested students. He had a great deal to offer, including many courses on a variety of psychic topics, including "psychospiritual transformation," and embracing your "shadow self".

They were exciting ideas, but all on a linear path of increasingly advanced topics. Before I could get to them, I would have to start at the beginning. This first step into the realm of remote viewing took me deep into the heart of the Catskill Mountains. Shrouded in an air of mystique, the precise location of our retreat must remain undisclosed. The only reason I was privy to it was thanks to Charlotte, who used her connections to help me gain access to this exclusive experience.

Immersed in the lush greenery, where the trees pierced

the sky and the air was filled with the soothing sounds of nature, we found ourselves in a secluded sanctuary. Here, the world as we knew it seemed to step back, and the boundaries between reality and the unseen thinned.

The course structure that unfolded over the following days was imbued with a disciplined and organized approach, reflective of its military origins, yet it thrived in harmony with the wilderness that enclosed us. We, a group of twenty curious souls, were comfortably lodged in a nearby hotel, further eliminating any distractions that could hamper our focus.

On the first day, we gathered in the hotel's conference room, equipped with state-of-the-art technology and well-stocked with food and beverages. Here, surrounded by fellow seekers, the adventure of delving into the mysteries of our minds was about to commence.

As we were handed our course manuals, a hefty volume labeled "Version 9", I couldn't help but feel a sense of intrigue. It held the names of all the participants, forming a tangible bond between us. Flipping through its pages, a quote from "Jonathan Livingston Seagull" caught my eye: "Break the chain of your thoughts... and you will break the chains of your body." It was as if these words were crafted just for me, fortifying my belief that I was exactly where I was meant to be.

David, our mentor on this extraordinary journey, emanated a powerful yet serene energy that instantly resonated with me. He embodied the qualities of a warrior monk, his military discipline seamlessly melded with a spiritual fervor, and his presence was a testament to the bridging of these two distinct worlds.

We commenced our exploration with a lecture on basic remote viewing theory, substantiated by real-world accounts and empirical evidence. As we delved deeper into these concepts, the seeds of this knowledge were sown in our minds, preparing us for the art of examining single points in space-time.

As grand as these ideas may seem, they are familiar to many people in one form or another. Thus, you might be amused to learn that this was the more "grounded" part of our lesson. After that, the lecture did what some might call "going off the deep end." For me, it was more like coming home. Topics included things such as "the 'I' of Infinite possibility," "a sea of photons," along with basic talks about momentum, energy, and how to transfer your perspective from particle to wave form.

David proved to be an extraordinary instructor. His teaching style was brimming with passion, deep knowledge, and experience. He was a remarkable teacher who used visual technology, exceptional presentation skills, and profound knowledge to keep his lessons both unique and engaging. Drifting beyond the topic of remote viewing, we learned about the heart, the mind, the human condition, and so much more.

While working with David, I learned of two subsets of remote viewing. First, there was coordinate remote viewing, or CRV, and the second was Advanced Remote Viewing, or ARV.

The technique I would be learning on this retreat,

coordinate remote viewing, was the method that was developed by the Stanford Research Institute, and was used in the U.S. Military's remote viewing program. CRV is without a doubt more rigidly structured than ARV.

Like the retreat's precise location, I must keep the intricate details, technique, and structure of this skill a secret, out of respect for David. I will, however, happily introduce you to the general concepts and setup of the process. If you think of the stages of CRV as the skeletal structure of learning remote viewing, David and his creative work would easily be the flesh and blood. For that reason, there are some of the details that I'm not at liberty to share in this book. Everyone in attendance promised to keep the specifics of David's training confidential, and it is a promise that we all honor to this day.

The viewer starts with a given set of coordinates or a coded target reference number, and then uses their intuitive perception to describe the target. Fascinatingly, the coordinates do not correspond to any actual geographic location; they are not longitude and latitude. Instead, they are merely a tool meant to serve as a mental prompt or focus.

The viewing's facilitator, in this case David, would put various details about the target inside of an envelope, typically photos or simply the name of a location. Along with that information would be a long, printed number. This is the coordinate number, the only information that the viewer is given before they travel to observe their target.

In the heart of the session, David delved into the

methodology behind remote viewing. He spoke about initiating the process with a deep state of relaxation, a kind of mental quietude that lets the mind detach from the surrounding physical reality. He then mentioned an obscure target, an item or a place, but left the specifics vague, as though purposefully shrouding it in mystery.

After achieving the right state of mind using David's methods, we were to reach out with our collective thoughts, venturing into the unknown while maintaining a firm anchor in the present. David emphasized the importance of careful observation, gently nudging us towards trusting our intuition and feelings as the mind explores unseen landscapes.

He talked about documenting the impressions, vague and fragmented as they might be. He suggested trusting the process, not judging or filtering what comes through, but allowing the mind to map its own journey.

An important aspect of the process was the necessity of analysis, but it should follow the explorative phase, not interrupt it. He maintained that revisiting impressions with a critical mindset was crucial to separating the wheat from the chaff, the insightful from the mundane.

The final step involved verifying the information, cross-referencing it with reality. However, David stressed that this was not a test of right or wrong but a process of understanding and aligning our perceptions.

I was beyond eager to get started on my first of many forays in remote viewing. Just beforehand, David confidently advised us: once we understand remote viewing, our perception of the world would never be the same. He even cautioned further that by merely comprehending the possibility of thinking beyond known limits, our individual lives would be irrevocably transformed.

This idea became apparent when I delved into my first session. The time for lecturing had concluded, and the time for viewing commenced. We were each given the same coordinate number for a single, shared envelope, and the session began. Each of us would be focused on the same target so that we could employ our collective consciousness in harvesting the details of the viewing.

Everyone donned eye masks, laid down on mats, and tried to relax. David moved us through guided meditation, using his own, custom-made music track and visualizations. His creative work was effective enough that, years later, I would still find myself listening to it.

The sound served to slow down our brainwaves to what is called "theta mind," also known simply as a deep, meditative state.

Theta waves are associated with deep states of meditation, often occurring in the hypnagogic state just before rapid eye movement (REM) sleep. These brainwave patterns, typically within a frequency range of 4-8 Hz, represent a significant slowing down of our brain activity.

This slowing is linked with the quieting of the conscious mind, a state that can lead to experiences of vivid imagery and sensations of expansion. In this state, we may find ourselves more receptive to intuitive insights, heightened creativity, and an enhanced ability for visualization.

This trance-like state can be induced through various techniques. Practices such as meditation, hypnosis, the use of rhythmic music or repetitive movements, guided visualization can all facilitate the transition into this state. Additionally, certain plant compounds or psychoactive substances can similarly prompt the onset of these theta brainwaves.

The therapeutic potential of these trance states of mind is significant. They promote healing, foster self-realization and self-exploration, and can even trigger spontaneous healing. By immersing ourselves in these theta-induced trance states, we can tap into deeper layers of our subconscious and open doors to inner growth and healing.

It is in this extraordinary state of mind that we become open to receive information through means other than our intellectual mind and conventional senses.

It took twenty to thirty minutes for the group to slow down our brain waves sufficiently to enter this hypnagogic state of mind. When we were there, the volume of the guiding music that assisted us in getting there was slowly reduced, until vanishing completely. At that time, we were directed to remove our eye masks and begin to write down information in the CRV format.

The program's manual guided us through the steps from the lecture. Again, out of respect for David's work, I am unable to go into great detail on these steps. But, in basic terms: we started with an "ideogram." This can be defined as a symbol or character in a writing system that represents a concept or an objective, rather than a specific word, or sound. Next, we recorded details of ascending specificity, describing emotions, perceptions, colors, textures, scent, tastes, temperature, sounds, and dimensions.

Following our individual journeys into the meditative state, we reconvened in a circle for a group discussion, known as "integration." In turn, each of us began to share our discoveries. We let the discussion unfold naturally over the course of an hour, allowing each participant to thoroughly delve into their perceptions and insights.

Once we had all shared, David prepared to reveal the target answers through a video presentation. This was the moment of truth, the chance to see how our individual experiences compared to the target that had been placed inside the envelope. As we watched, a rich discussion ensued as we related each piece of information to one that a viewer had gleaned while in a meditative state.

In addition to the collective exchange of knowledge, there was one other thing that the entire group had the pleasure of sharing—mutual excitement at what we had accomplished through a process that was genuinely enjoyable.

Of course, I am unable to share the specifics of what I intuited from the exercise and how they compared to the contents of my envelope. However, although it's difficult to quantify due to the subjective nature of my perceptions, I can admit that my first effort returned a humble sixty percent accuracy. By traditional academic standards, that's

1% above a failing grade.

But, I was okay with that. In fact, I was thrilled. After all, I wasn't there to pick up a new trick and ace it on day one. Like everything else, the skill of remote viewing required practice. Throughout the week, the information I returned with became increasingly accurate.

Each following day, we repeated the process, starting with a lecture about theory, history, and of most interest to me: spiritual, philosophical, and inspirational content. After this, we would have another practice session, followed by discussion and integration. The material in the manual was like a spiritual bible to me. I felt privileged to even be glimpsing at this tome that was abundant with secrets of the universe. Even in the off-hours of the course, I never grew tired of reading it, exploring it.

With each passing day, we went deeper into our non-ordinary states, and we returned with increasingly accurate information. After performing two sessions per day for five days straight, the results made it clear to all of us that we were capable of intuiting information through space and time. A personal highlight was several of us in the group being able to access Ted. They could describe his look, sound, words and mannerisms without ever having 'met' him.

This further solidified my faith in the connected web of our universe, and the potential of our mind to tap into a reality beyond physical sight. Breaking free of our perceived limitations, being open to listen to another intelligence, trusting that the unknown can be known: remote viewing showed me another aspect of what is possible when we tap into a non ordinary state of mind.

As the first one-week program drew to a close, my appetite for remote viewing remained insatiable. Typically, his students would return every six months or so to complete one class at a time over the course of many years. I, however, still had a roaring flame of curiosity within me, so I opted for a more direct path.

"How quickly can you teach me everything that you offer?" I asked.

David told me that he ran a new course every couple months. If I attended every single one, I could reach his highest level of education within one year. It was a process that I happily and promptly agreed to.

I still had a few weeks to wait for another chance to learn from David, but I wasn't exactly in the waiting mode. Instead, I reached out to Charlotte to ask for more guidance on how I could continue my studies. This was how I learned of a place known as the Monroe Institute, which held many wonders of its own.

The Monroe Institute

Joseph was a retired U.S. Army NCO and Chief Warrant Officer. He was one of the original officers recruited for the top-secret program that David was eventually brought into —Stargate and Grill Flame. During his time there, he is reported to have carried out thousands of remote viewing sessions.

After retiring from the Army, Joseph began, among other things, teaching as a guest instructor at the Monroe Institute, a non-profit research and educational organization devoted to the exploration of human consciousness. The institute itself was founded by Robert Monroe, who was known for his work in out-of-body experiences. McMoneagle's work there involved a wide range of fields, which happened to include applications of remote viewing and consciousness development.

To me, the Monroe Institute was a playground for consciousness, and I wanted to spread myself across the countless programs they had available. There was one called "Journey to T-cells" for people who needed to balance their immune system. Then there were others like

"Opening the Way" for mothers who were anxious about giving birth and bringing life into the world, and "Going Home," which explored death itself.

As it turned out, I would first need to enter a program called "Gateway Exploration," a foundational course that was required of participants before they were allowed to advance to higher-level work. It was designed to help participants explore a vast array of states of consciousness. At the basic level, the Gateway Exploration was designed to help us learn to enter, explore, and utilize various states of consciousness to access guidance, problem-solve, heal, and enhance our lives. All of these events had frequent overlap with out-of-body experiences.

I learned that the program uses its own, unique, patented audio technology known as Hemi-Sync. The name was short for hemispheric synchronization, a technique that uses binaural beats to encourage specific states of mind.

By now, the concept and employment of binaural beats has become relatively mainstream, with free tracks easily findable on sites like Youtube and Spotify. At the time, though, they were a much more niche practice. Although I can't speak to the legitimacy, efficacy, or the adequacy of consumer-grade headphones to deliver free tracks from the internet, I can now say for certain that The Monroe Institute offered "the real deal."

Gateway exploration was a one-week program, designed like many retreats with full room and board provided. Soon enough I was packing my things to pay the

Monroe Institute a visit.

The drive from South Carolina to Virginia took me through the Blue Ridge Mountains, which was one of my favorite routes, particularly during autumn. The color of the leaves made for breathtaking and soul-nourishing scenery. I was feeling wonderful, and I hadn't even left the state yet. That was how I knew I was heading in the right direction.

Eventually, I pulled off of Interstate 64 at the Afton exit, and completed the last leg of the journey along the winding, and increasingly beautiful, Robert Mountain Road—named after the institute's founder. Upon arrival, I was met with a sense of peace and tranquility, which is saying a lot considering the serene state the drive itself had put me in.

The campus was situated on over 300 acres of rolling hills, boasting panoramic mountain views. Inside, a pleasant greeter met me at reception and showed me to a building dubbed the Nancy Penn Center, which was designed to accommodate 24 guests.

Inside, I was brought to my accommodations—a private chamber equipped with a small bed, bathroom, closet space, cutting-edge sound system, headset, and eye-mask. I learned that the room itself would double as a session space, where I would listen to guided meditations and program facilitators through headphones. A two way communication system was also installed so that we could contact our facilitators if needed. The space was designed to be simply comfortable and adequately equipped for its purposes, nothing more. It was strange to be standing in a room that seemed so stark and vacant, while at the same time being full of potential.

Each moment that passed between me and the official start of the retreat was defined by my excitement to surrender, open my mind fully, learn, experience, and grow. After settling into my assigned room, I left to explore the facility.

The first wonder I encountered was two enormous rose quartz crystals, weighing about 6 tons each. I felt welcomed not only by the energy emanating from the crystal, but also the energy of the space itself. Historical photos of the institute's founding years adorned the wall, telling the story of the events that lead up to this very moment.

Of course, out of respect for the institute, I can't go into detail on the session itself, but when it concluded, similar to David's program, we were required to gather in the Integration Hall. Here, we sat in a circle to share and discuss our experiences. This was also my first time meeting the group as a whole, which was enthralling in and of itself. We had all come from unique walks of life. They were not psychics or clairvoyants or magicians. They were people like you and me: doctors, artists, scientists, journalists, and teachers.

There was also a plethora of unique motives for being there. Some people were participating because they were driven by some form of curiosity—either inward personal expansion, or outward exploration. Others were encountering shifts in their lives, and looking to shape their transition into something that set them up for success in their next phase of existence, whatever it may be. Personally, I wanted to sate my curiosity about life after death. Where did people go? What was on the other side?

After a few days, it became clear that attending these sessions in my private space would be one of the most rewarding activities for my brain and mind. Every morning, we would rise between 5 and 6 AM. Breakfast was prepared for us in the dining room, made entirely of healthy, organic, and local food.

After breakfast, we would start at the teaching hall for a briefing on what the day held in store. Then, we would listen to lectures or teaching from our facilitator or a guest speaker. Immediately following that, each participant would return to their bed, also lovingly called a portal, and commence our next forays into the vast unknown.

Next, we would all reunite for another integration before breaking for lunch, typically enjoying it in a beautiful garden, beneath delightful sunshine. After another session of viewing and integration, we were given the rest of the afternoon to relax, walk, or go on a local hike—all activities which drove further contemplation of our experiences. After dinner, a night session was offered before bed. This time, no integration would be held, and we would instead carry our findings into a deep and restful sleep.

It was a cumulative experience, and it felt like we were in a trance-like state throughout the week. There were no cell phones, no external interruptions—only the pure essence of being present in the here-and-now. We were in a psychedelic state of mind without the use of any substances, instead simply harnessing the power of sound, frequency, and vibration. When it comes to rejuvenation, this was an experience that facilitated both personal and spiritual growth.

It was an exceedingly well-designed program that gradually took us deeper and deeper into understanding the universe beyond our minds, handing us keys to the cosmic locks for our journeys, while also providing a utopian haven for us to return to between sessions.

The property was immense, and it contained everything that we could have wanted—a swimming pool, garden, lawn, forests, and hiking trail. All of it was speckled with places to sit and contemplate our findings. On top of hiking, we were invited to participate in activities like tai chi, qigong, and simple, serene reading. I stayed on the institute's grounds from the first second of the retreat to the last.

It felt as though cultivating a non-ordinary mindset was not strictly limited to the confines of our sessions and integrations. Instead, it was twenty-four hours a day, from the moment my eyes opened, to when they closed, and through every dream I had—I remained in some degree of a non-ordinary state of mind the entire time.

At the end of that first week, naturally, I signed up for every single course that the institute had to offer. It was a path of study that would require four years to complete, with a few weeks to months in-between to pursue other interests, complete another one of David's courses, and enjoy other means of expanding my mind.

In contemplating remote viewing, I draw from various

wellsprings of knowledge—from quantum physics to neuroscience, from philosophy to spirituality. It's like piecing together a grand puzzle, where each piece sheds light on a different facet of the phenomenon.

The human mind, with its manifold layers and uncharted pathways, has fascinated me ever since I can remember. I view it as an intricate puzzle box, the solution to which yields an understanding of ourselves, our reality, and our potential. My experiences with Dr. Morehouse as well as the Monroe Institute were major waypoints in this journey.

To me, remote viewing appears as a powerful testament to the hidden capabilities of our minds. As an experience, it transcends the bounds of our everyday reality, transporting us through space and time. As a practice, it requires dedication, concentration, and an open mind willing to perceive without bias. It's like learning to tune into a frequency, a cosmic radio station, where the broadcasts are snapshots of distant places and times.

This phenomenon of remote viewing seems beyond the reach of contemporary science to explain fully. Yet, the intersection of multiple theories and principles, many of which lie in the domain of neuroscience, might hint at possible explanations.

Consciousness and quantum mechanics seem to dance in an intimate ballet. Quantum theory's tenets, particularly quantum entanglement with its implication of immediate information transfer regardless of distance, aligns harmoniously with my experiences of remote viewing. It's as if the phenomenon harnesses the quantum interconnectedness of everything, allowing us to perceive information otherwise beyond our reach.

Further, I believe in the concept of the non-locality of consciousness. This idea proposes that consciousness extends beyond the physical confines of the brain, much like a magnetic field stretches beyond the magnet. It's an invigorating thought—the mind as a field connecting us all, capable of accessing information from anywhere within that field. This framework lends remote viewing a theoretical foundation, one that's consistent with my experiences.

Neuroscience suggests that our right brain hemisphere is responsible for holistic thinking and intuition. This hemisphere could be an essential participant in remote viewing, integrating the distant information into a coherent whole. It's as if our right hemisphere acts as a radio receiver, tuned to the subtle signals of the universe.

I also find a connection between neural oscillations and remote viewing. Brain waves such as theta waves, often associated with states of deep relaxation and creativity, appear to foster an open, receptive mind. During remote viewing, I believe that our brains might tap into these frequencies, thus providing a neural environment conducive to psychic perception.

In my musings, I've also considered the role of mirror neurons—the 'empathy neurons,' as some call them. I see a possible correlation between these neurons, which fire in response to both performed and observed actions, and the empathetic connection formed during remote viewing. Perhaps these neurons assist in forming a neural bridge between the viewer and the observed.

Another intriguing concept is transliminal brain functioning. This idea proposes that psychic phenomena may occur due to an increase in information flow across the brain's threshold of awareness. In my opinion, this concept fits snugly with the practice of remote viewing, suggesting that we may perceive more than our conscious mind ordinarily allows.

Finally, my contemplations led me to consider the role of psychedelics. These substances, known to alter consciousness dramatically, often induce a state of hyper-connectivity in the brain. Users frequently report experiences of unity, interconnectedness, and profound understanding, echoing some qualities of remote viewing. Could psychedelics provide a temporary doorway, opening up pathways to information usually hidden from our conscious minds? I sometimes wonder if these experiences enable our brain to break free from its usual boundaries, allowing us to dip our toes into the vast ocean of universal consciousness.

Even with these theories, I'm aware that my understanding of remote viewing remains incomplete. It's like trying to grasp the vast expanse of the night sky with a telescope; no matter how powerful, the instrument can only reveal a fraction of the whole. And yet, the thrill of the quest, the allure of the unknown, and the ecstasy of occasional discovery keep me on this journey, eager for whatever insight the next turn might offer.

The fascinating realm of remote viewing is not limited to perceiving physical objects or events at a distance. It extends into an equally intriguing domain known as remote healing, a practice that has shown much potential in recent years. Dr. Julia Mossbridge, in her groundbreaking book 'The Premonition Code,' delves deep into the scientific realm of precognition. Her work reveals a startling truth: that sensing the future can indeed be possible. As a skilled remote viewer herself, Dr. Mossbridge offers profound insights into remote healing. She emphasizes the necessity to attain an extraordinary or non-ordinary state of consciousness—a specific mental state that allows us to access or even alter the programming of our sentient beings.

Various techniques exist to induce these non-ordinary states of consciousness that allow for remote healing. Medical qigong meditation, for instance, utilizes guided visualizations. This technique consciously introduces information into the mind during an extraordinary state, paving the way for profound transformation and healing.

Similarly, the Monroe Institute, renowned for its pioneering work in consciousness exploration, offers various programs aimed at healing and consciousness expansion. Their healing program, the 'Journey to T Cells,' and their remote viewing curriculum all utilize guided visualization techniques. In these programs, the visualization serves to influence cellular functions, stimulate immune balance, or access sought-after information via remote viewing.

This extraordinary state of mind—a gateway into the realm of remote viewing and healing—is not an exclusive domain accessible only to a select few. It is an innate human capacity that we can *all* learn to tap into, refine, and utilize. This state of mind offers a unique conduit into the energetic fabric of our reality and ourselves—a pathway through which we can realize profound transformation and healing.

However, it is crucial to note that while remote healing presents intriguing possibilities, it should not replace conventional healthcare but rather complement it. This emerging field is part of a larger topic encompassing healing and recovery, which we will explore in greater depth later in this book.

As we delve deeper into our exploration of non-ordinary states of consciousness, we expand our understanding of the extraordinary capacities inherent within us. It is my hope that this discussion serves as an invitation for you to embark on your own exploration—whether that be within the realm of remote viewing, remote healing, or beyond— to discover what lies beyond the boundaries of ordinary awareness.

For those willing to dig deep into the mysteries of the universe, one possible explanation for remote viewing and healing may lie within what I refer to as the Matrix Field. This concept resonates with the theories put forth by visionaries like Nassim Haramein, who propose a unified field at the quantum level—an all-pervasive cosmic web that connects every form of life and consciousness across space and time.

The Matrix Field, in essence, can be likened to a universal holographic projection where each point in the universe contains information about the whole. This idea is reminiscent of the principles of holography, where every fragment of a holographic film contains the entire image.

Within the context of this Matrix Field, particles separated by vast expanses of space and time can form instantaneous connections, thereby creating a vast information network that transcends our conventional understanding of space-time constraints. Such a field provides an information superhighway that facilitates phenomena like remote viewing and healing.

This notion aligns with the principle of nonlocality in quantum physics, where particles that have interacted in the past can remain instantaneously connected no matter how far apart they are. Nonlocality challenges our everyday perception of the world, providing a scientific basis for phenomena like remote viewing that seem impossible within our everyday, classical worldview.

Thus, the Matrix Field represents an immense repository of information that extends far beyond our typical sensory perception. It's akin to an endless reservoir of knowledge, waiting for us to tap into its depths. By accessing this field, we can tap into information that is otherwise inaccessible through our conventional senses.

Yet, as we dive deeper into these extraordinary realms of consciousness, we must bear in mind the responsibility that comes with such explorations. While these non-ordinary states can provide profound insights and transformative experiences, they must be approached with respect, caution, and an intent centered on growth, healing, and understanding.

A different perspective that may explain the efficacy of remote viewing, remote healing, and other similar phenomena is the concept of the Source—a term used to describe an ultimate, higher power within a spiritual context. The Source is often perceived as the fountainhead of consciousness, the singularity from which everything springs into existence. It's seen as the dynamic, primal energy that fuels the universe, sparking the creation of all life forms.

Throughout history and across different cultures, belief systems, and traditions, this concept has been referred to by many names—God, the Divine, the Origin, to name just a few. Despite its varied labels, it consistently symbolizes the very essence of life and the nucleus of all creation. Yet, understanding the Source is an intensely personal and subjective journey, its meaning influenced by a multitude of factors like culture, tradition, and individual spiritual outlook. For most, it symbolizes an entity or state that surpasses our own mortal existence, linking us to a higher, transcendental reality.

The Source underscores the inherent interconnectedness of all beings and aspects of the universe. However, unlike a direct connection through the Matrix Field, this connection is mediated via a higher entity, state, or realm. This belief in a supreme power of limitless wisdom can guide our paths, inspire our spirits, and instill in us the courage to venture into the unknown. It can direct us towards leading a life suffused with a deeper sense of meaning and purpose.

Thus, I introduce the Source as a philosophical

framework that propels us to explore not only the nature of reality but also our individual spirituality and our interconnectedness with the world that surrounds us. It serves as a powerful catalyst for personal transformation, inspiring us to continually grow, adapt, and evolve—all of which are critical when undertaking practices like remote viewing. For many, delving into the concept of the Source signifies a pivotal shift in their perspective and approach to life—a profound transformation that echoes the transformative power of practices like remote viewing.

When guiding individuals on their journey through remote viewing, I emphasize the significance of fully activating all senses. I encourage them to absorb information in its purest, most unadulterated form—unobscured by personal biases and preconceptions. Before embarking on this exploratory journey, I share a fundamental principle: for successful engagement with remote viewing, it's essential to let go of our entrenched selfhood, to open our minds and accept information from a neutral, unattached state of consciousness. We need to discard our mental "rolodex"—our accumulated past experiences, our ingrained patterns of thought and perception.

This mindset is not only vital for Controlled Remote Viewing (CRV), it's a perspective that can radically shift how we engage with the world in our everyday lives. It requires a mental metamorphosis—abandoning our customary view of the world and embracing a novel outlook, one that perceives the world as it truly is, stripped of our personal biases and narratives. This shift can be both illuminating and transformative, offering a fascinating new lens through which we can observe and engage with reality.

Through adopting this unique perspective, we step out of our individual selves and our subjective experiences, entering a realm of unbiased observation and raw data intake. We attune our senses to the vast symphony of the universe, listening to its melodies and harmonies with fresh ears and seeing its intricate patterns with new eyes. This transformative shift not only enhances our capacity for remote viewing but also cultivates a profound sense of connection and unity with the world around us. It's an invaluable tool in our pursuit of understanding the Matrix Field, the Source, and the grand fabric of existence they compose.

Andean Shaman

My voracious appetite to learn more on the topic of remote viewing simply could not be quelled. I was driven by a simple intention: to delve deeper into the collective consciousness and foster spiritual transformation. If modern day people were able to pursue this discipline, what had ancient cultures been capable of? During times of being closer to nature and unrestricted by electronic devices, what wonders could those minds behold?

David had spent a great deal of time learning about indigenous cultures who were believed to have traveled through space and time by unknown means. Specifically, he had been impressed with what he saw in the Andes, Bolivia, and Machu Picchu. As you can imagine, when he told me he was planning for the first time to bring a group to explore this exciting world, I was the first to sign up.

An exploration like this was the perfect continuation for my previous journeys in remote viewing. There was a delightful synchronicity between learning these skills and exploring a sacred region of many mysteries which modern science struggles to explain. From the remarkable architecture in Machu Picchu, to evidence that the indigenous people were communicating with other parts of the world despite their isolation in the mountains.

The journey turned out to be a life-changing exploration, brimming with unexpected and wonderful surprises from the unknown.

Before leaving, David informed us that this trip would be different from most guided trips. He knew that many people from western cultures preferred organization and preparation. The question "what's next?" was frequently on their lips, and any gap in knowledge that hindered preparation did nothing but cause stress. This trip, much like the darkness retreat, would require trust, and we would have to completely relinquish control of our journey.

Going into the trip, my knowledge of the indigenous inhabitants of the Andean region during ancient times was fairly limited. I was more familiar with the stunning archaeological sites such as Machu Picchu. To me, the region stood as a symbol of rich cultural diversity. Its geographical locations alone—encompassing high altitudes, equatorial latitudes, expansive coastal deserts, and lush rainforests—spoke volumes of the unique experiences that awaited me there.

Following a short flight from Lima, we arrived in Cusco, Peru, on a brilliantly sunny day. Most of the people on the trip, myself absolutely included, grappled with the symptoms of altitude sickness. Traveling to a city that was situated 11,000 feet above sea level translated to lethargy, headaches, fatigue, and nausea.

The entire group had one vital ally in the battle against these symptoms—raw excitement for the exploration that lay ahead. The trip promised a wealth of learning opportunities that we were all eager to delve into. To support further suppression of altitude sickness, I was treated to my first experience with local medicine.

My knowledge of medicinal plants and shamanic practices was rather limited, but upon chewing coca leaves, as well as drinking coca tea, I received quite the education. Their power over the symptoms was undeniable. I learned that Coca leaves had been used for thousands of years by indigenous communities in the Andean region for this purpose and many others. In addition to alleviating altitude sickness, the leaves were used in various religious rituals, and even to overcome hunger and thirst.

This is because Coca leaves contain several alkaloids which have a mild stimulant effect, similar to caffeine. The result is improving the consumer's ability to absorb oxygen into their bloodstream, which is particularly valuable in the thin air of higher altitudes.

Our main contact there was Jorge Luis Delgado, the Andean Shaman who had first opened David's eyes to the wonders of the place. He was born in the highland near lake Titicaca in the community of Aymara, which we would be visiting later in our trip. The Aymara people had a rich cultural heritage, with traditions and practices that predated the Incan Empire.

Jorge's title of "Andean Shaman" carried a wide range of meanings. It refers to a spiritual healer or practitioner from anywhere in the Andean Region of South America, including Peru, Ecuador, Bolivia, Columbia, and parts of Argentina and Chile. Essentially, Shamanism involves interaction with a spirit world through non-ordinary states of consciousness—definitely my cup of tea.

In terms of healing, Andean shamans may perform various types of rituals using techniques like energy medicine, soul retrieval, divination, and plant medicine. These methods often incorporate natural elements like herbs, stones, incense, condor feathers, chanting, and praying. The most common of these rituals involve offering to Pachamama, or mother nature, and the Apus, or spiritual deities, to express gratitude, ask for blessings, and bring balance to our relationship with the natural world.

As for non-ordinary states of mind, these include trance-states that sometimes occur when a person is meditating and their brainwaves are at the theta frequency, the hypnagogic, pre-dream state that I mentioned earlier. So, Jorge wasn't simply a guide for our tour through the region, he was in fact respected as an intermediary between the human and spirit worlds, a modern-day Inca who walked a spiritual path.

After one night in Cusco, we got into a bus and headed for Lake Titicaca, located in the city of Puno, it is a place of deep spiritual significance for the Andean peoples, as many ancient ruins can be found around the lake, including the famous Tiwanaku, a pre-Inca archeological site.

The lake itself is one of South America's largest lakes, measuring over three thousand square miles, and the highest navigable body of water in the world, sitting at over 12,500 feet above sea level. It straddles the border between Peru and Bolivia.

Perhaps one of the most striking images of Lake Titicaca is it's "Floating Islands," built by the Uros people. There are many places that empty fanciful adjectives in their names—the Glass Beach in California, Rainbow Mountains in China, and even the Floating Islands in Dubai.

None of these are meant to be taken literally, which is exactly what sets the Uros floating islands apart from the norm. They were artificial islands made from totora reed, a buoyant plant that grows abundantly in the shallows of the lake. The islands do, quite literally, float on the water. They're wide and stable enough to host housing, and anchored with ropes that are attached to stakes which have been driven into the bottom of the lake to prevent the islands from drifting away. The reeds are interwoven in such a way that they form a solid and stable surface for the Uros people.

The Uros people permanently lived on the islands, constantly adding new reeds to the surface while the bottom layers rot and disintegrate in the water. So, why not simply live on dry land? Why go through the trouble? I was fascinated to learn that the Uros people constructed these floating islands for defensive purposes. The ability to move the islands provided a unique form of protection against potential threats. If conflict arose, they could cut the anchoring ropes and move their entire village to a safer location.

Living on these floating islands also allowed the Uros people to maintain a distinct cultural identity and way of life. The isolation allowed them to preserve their traditions, customs, and language despite the encroaching, more dominant cultures.

After two days on the lake, I was offered an opportunity to take part in something called a "Vine Ceremony." With a little explanation, I soon understood that this was about to be my first experience with the psychedelic compound known as ayahuasca. It was tremendously exciting, especially considering the "surprise" factor. Afterall, I had not come here seeking this experience. Instead, I felt as though it had found me.

However, there is so much to be said about ayahuasca, and I still have a great deal of the Andean Region to show you. If you will indulge me, reader, I would like to embrace the nonlinear nature of time that tends to accompany non-ordinary states of mind. Let us pass by the pocket dimension of my first ayahuasca experience for now, and offer a promise that we'll return to it when the time is right.

After the ceremony, it was time for us to move on toward other sacred sites on our way back to Cusco. The first of these sites was Sacsayhuaman, a location with a name that is difficult to interpret in written form, but once you hear it spoken, you never forget it. Not a single person on the trip could resist letting out a slight giggle when we learned that the pronunciation sounded almost identical to "sexy woman".

Sacsayhuaman is well-known for its massive, intricately laid stone walls. Some of the individual stones used in the construction of these walls weigh as much as 200 tons, yet they are fitted together with such precision that it's often said not even a piece of paper can be slipped between them.

The largest structure within the complex is often called "The Fortress" due to its size and the thickness of its walls, although it is unclear whether or not it was intended to serve a defensive purpose. Jorge also shared with us that it was used as a ceremonial site in the past. We meditated there, seeking information from our collective consciousness through remote viewing. Although historians state that this site was constructed around the middle of the 15th century, the consensus among us was that it could have been built much earlier than is recorded in the history books.

Our adventure continued and at this point I must say, I would be terribly remiss if I didn't speak about the local food—especially considering its unorthodox form. Exploring the rich tapestry of Peru's culinary landscape was as much a journey as the physical trek itself. One of the most intriguing experiences was trying an indigenous delicacy known as 'mud'—an edible clay consumed by the locals.

This practice, known as geophagy, is common in numerous traditional cultures globally. The clay I tasted was a type known as "chaco," a staple typically paired with potatoes. This tradition, which predates the arrival of the Spanish, is attributed to the clay's detoxifying properties, as it's believed to bind to plant toxins. The clay, when consumed with potatoes, assists in neutralizing harmful substances like glycoalkaloids found in some Andean potato varieties.

In addition to its detoxifying effects, chaco also supplies essential minerals and can provide relief from indigestion. The traditional preparation involves boiling peeled potatoes then dipping them into a sauce made from the clay mixed with water, sometimes seasoned with salt or other flavors. A seemingly unusual combination, yet the taste was oddly satisfying.

Throughout the journey, our meals were wholesome and delicious. We often savored the taste of locally sourced rainbow trout from nearby rivers, typically grilled or fried. Boiled yellow potatoes, served cold with a slightly spicy, creamy sauce made of cheese, peruvian yellow chili, condensed milk, olives, and boiled egg, were a delight.

This dish, which hails from Huancayo in the Andean highlands of Peru, became a favorite. Simple yet flavorful meals such as Choclo con quest were also a treat—a large-kernel variety of corn served with slices of fresh cheese, often sold by street vendors.

Although the locals' diet includes meats like guinea pig, alpaca, chicken, and beef, my dietary preferences led me down a different path. For decades, I have identified as a flexitarian, consuming mostly plant-based foods and abstaining from meat. However, my diet does include small sea creatures and eggs.

Quenching the thirst from our hikes, Chicha Morada, a traditional non-alcoholic beverage made of purple corn, pineapple, cinnamon, and clove, became our constant companion. It's ubiquitous across Pero and refreshingly sweet, an ideal drink for a weary traveler. Through the culinary lens, the journey through the andes was as much a feast for the palate as it was for the soul.

As the trip progressed, I had the opportunity to get to know Jorge more, and come to a deeper understanding of his beliefs. The Aymara belief system is syncretic, combining traditional Andean spiritual beliefs with elements of Roman Catholicism. They believe in the Pachamama, known in English simply as Mother Earth. Pachamama is seen as a conscious entity with whom we can interact, and whose balance and wellbeing is critical to all life. They also believe in cosmology, where the universe is seen as divided into three interconnected realms.

The Hanan Pacha is the upper world, the realm of gods and celestial beings. It's associated with the sky, the sun, the moon, stars, and planets. It represents the spiritual world and is traditionally symbolized by the condor in Incan mythology.

Kay Pacha is the middle world, or the world of the living. This realm is associated with human beings, animals, and plants. It's essentially the Earth as we know it, and is connected to the daily life and experiences of people. It's traditionally symbolized by the puma, representing strength and terrestrial power.

Lastly, Uku Pacha is the inner world, or underworld. This realm is associated with the inner life of the Earth, the world of the dead, ancestors, and the unknown. It symbolizes the world beneath the surface, including the soil and the oceans. It is traditionally symbolized by the snake or serpent.

Fascinated by the layers of Andean spiritual practices, I listened intently as Jorge elaborated on the intricate distinction between Andean Shamans and Andean priests. These roles, steeped in rich cultural history and tradition, vary widely within the scope of Andean society. Both provide unique perspectives on spirituality.

Contrasting to the shamanic role of being spiritual intermediaries between humans and the higher, spiritual realms, Andean priests often align more closely with formal religious infrastructures. The most common of these structures is the Catholic Church, which has maintained significant sway over the region since the era of Spanish colonization.

Tasked with leading communal worship, conducting ceremonies, and imparting religious teachings, they play a pivotal role in maintaining the spiritual harmony of their communities. Their authority is commonly anchored in their ordination within the church, guided by an established framework of religious doctrines that steer their practices and beliefs.

Recognizing the unique roles of shamans and priests seemed a crucial step in truly understanding the spiritual landscape in Andean culture. The intricate interplay between their distinct paths lended depth and dimension to local traditions, underscoring the diverse spiritual tapestry of the region.

The knowledge Jorge imparted on me was stimulating to the imagination and spirit, but much greater experiences awaited me in the remainder of the trip. Jorge was about to bring us to places where we could see, and indeed interact with, the spirit world he had told us of thus far.

The Doorway

Our journey continued to our next stop, the breathtaking Urubamba Valley. This stretch of wonder, colloquially known as the Sacred Valley. Despite technically being a valley, it was actually nestled among the tower heights of Peru's majestic highlands, about six-thousand feet above sea level.

The Urubamba Valley was greatly cherished by the Incan civilization due to its unique geographical features and favorable climatic conditions. These two factors intertwined to foster an environment rich for agricultural prosperity. Indeed, the Sacred Valley was the Inca Empire's powerhouse for maize production - a vital crop in their society.

Strategically positioned at the heart of the Inca Empire, the Sacred Valley was more than just a farmland. It served as a crucial link on the route to the dense jungle, and the empire's primary source for the cultivation of coca leaves, which played an integral role in Inca society for traditional medicine and religious rituals.

As we explored the area, I appreciated that the Sacred Valley was far from a forgotten relic of the past. It was still vibrant and teeming with life because many indigenous communities continue to call the place home. Among them were the Quechua-speaking people, proud descendants of the Inca civilization. Holding steadfast to their ancestral roots, they maintained a traditional lifestyle that had been passed down through generations. Agriculture still played a central role, and the skillful art of weaving, along with other crafts, was practiced with a level of mastery that can only be achieved through centuries of accumulated practice.

In essence, our visit to the Sacred Valley was more than just a stop on the journey to Machu Picchu. It was a profound step back in time, a living tapestry of a rich cultural heritage. It was a place where the echoes of the past resonated strongly with me, creating a truly unforgettable experience.

Leaving the Urubamba Valley, our journey continued under the guidance of Jorge as he led us to another remarkable destination—a valley bathed in the glow of pink sandstones. The panorama that unfolded before our eyes was strikingly unusual; rock clusters had been sculpted by the whims of nature into intriguing formations. Some bore the semblance of animals, others shaped like mystical gateways or ancient temples. A few even mirrored human faces frozen in a variety of expressions. The surreal landscape seemed to be teasing our imaginations, constantly changing its guise as we navigated deeper into its confines.

Our trail took us to a towering, monolithic rock wall. We trod the path with reverence, honoring the deep bond the locals had formed with the surrounding nature. Our climb became steeper, and we found ourselves funneled through a narrow passage. After what felt like a timeless traverse, we reached our destination, a monumental stone which Jorge called the "portal," or "doorway."

This doorway, shrouded in the mystique of local legends, was infamous for the sporadic disappearances reported in its vicinity. In accord with the sacredness of the site, it was a tradition to seek permission from the spirit guardian that was believed to preside over the area. So, just as our shaman did, we each followed suit, silently asking for consent to approach.

What stood before us was a massive stone wall, and an indentation carved out in the form of a door. It was a majestic spectacle, wide enough to accommodate the span of two outstretched arms, and tall enough to frame an average person. This was the Door of Aramu Muru.

In a moment of shared silence, I stepped into the carved space, standing in the doorway, both my arms spread wide, my forehead and chest pressed against the cool, ancient stone. The world fell away. I was enveloped in an overwhelming sense of serenity, a profound calmness seeping into my heart and pacifying my racing thoughts. The feeling was akin to a mild psychoactive state, a sense of detachment from the physical realm and a connection to something larger. Perhaps this is clear without saying, but, it was a beautiful and truly mystical experience.

Jorge spoke up, his voice softly breaking the tranquility

that had surrounded us. He explained that the Doorway of Aramu Muru was not just a physical structure, but a bridge, a conduit designed to connect consciousnesses. As I stood there, at the threshold of the unknown, I felt a shift within myself—an understanding, a connection that transcended the physical world. It was a deeply personal, transformative experience, one that I will carry with me forever.

Soon, it was time to move on to the climactic final stop of our trip—Machu Picchu. As we approached our destination, I could feel that something special was waiting for me. Emerging from the foliage of the Peruvian Andes, the mystical citadel unfolded before us. Renowned as one of the world's most awe-inspiring archaeological sites, Machu Picchu stands as a lasting testament to the engineering prowess and architectural mastery of the Inca civilization. Yet even today, the precise methods of its construction remain cloaked in a shroud of mystery.

Built in the 15th century during the zenith of the Inca empire, Machu Picchu is among the rare pre-Columbian ruins that have largely escaped the ravages of time. The site, symbolic of indigenous ingenuity and resilience, holds significant cultural importance for the local Quechua people and the nation of Peru.

Perched in the rugged highlands of the Andes, Machu Picchu is a marvel of engineering. The Incas, with no access to modern technology or even the wheel, constructed monumental structures using ashlar—or dry-stone—masonry. Stones were meticulously cut to fit together without mortar, many of which remain steadfast and unyielding even after centuries. This exacting precision also fortified the structures against earthquakes, the stones capable of slight movement before settling back into their original places.

Despite the absence of draft animals for carrying substantial loads and the non-usage of wheels for transport, the Incas orchestrated an astonishing feat of construction. It's believed that hundreds, if not thousands of men labored to move the massive stones, likely employing ropes, ramps, and a complex system of levers.

Yet, as we observed Machu Picchu, as well as the multitude of other sacred sites we had visited on our journey, our collective consciousness stirred with speculation. Some of these grand structures, their construction methods continuing to baffle modern architects and engineers, could well predate the Inca era. Messages and images emerged in our minds, possibly products of our imagination, or perhaps echoes of a distant past, suggesting that these archaeological marvels could be as ancient as 25,000 to 40,000 years old.

The very thought of it provoked a wave of profound reflection. When we contemplate the construction of Machu Picchu, we are faced with questions that modern science struggles to satisfactorily answer. Could the civilizations of that time have been vastly different from our current Homo sapiens? Could they have harnessed different technologies to erect these remarkable structures? Might their means of communication and transportation have diverged dramatically from ours?

Contemplating these possibilities lent an even deeper

sense of mystery to the historical depths of humanity. Machu Picchu was not merely an archeological wonder—it was a fascinating enigma, a mirror to the potential complexities of our past, enticing us to delve deeper into the labyrinth of human history.

We arrived at our housing for the night, a boutique hotel nestled in Aguas Calientes at the base of Machu Picchu called Casa del Sol Machupicchu. The lodging, as with every prior stop, was quaint and rustic. The outward beauty of the area was perfectly embodied within the building's interior, which was lush with nature. We were quick to sleep that night, because the following morning would be an early one.

We embarked on our journey at 4 AM and hiked for more than an hour, ascending higher into the mountains. As we came to a narrow ridge, and I was reminded of the darkness retreat when we were instructed to walk single file with our eyes closed, holding hands with the people ahead of and behind us. A narrow mountain trail might be the last place you would want to keep your eyes open, but I thought that my practice in trusting the darkness would make the process easy.

As it turned out, I was engaging in a completely different exercise. The darkness retreat had prepared me for the psychological effects of the uncertainty that game with blindness, but it had not taught me to quell the physiological effects. Goosebumps rose on my skin. My heartbeat rose occasionally with the wind, or when I envisioned the great depths below us. We kept walking for what felt like the longest, most thrilling ten minutes of my life.

The leader of the line halted, and we all followed suit. Jorge's voice broke the silences, instructing us to remain still and keep our eyes closed while he led us in a morning meditation. We paid respects to Pachamama and the Apus, expressed gratitude to ourselves, to our loved ones, and to all those who were within reach of our love.

When all was silent again, our wonderful shaman directed us to open our eyes, revealing one of the most incredible sights of the trip. I beheld the sparkling glow of the morning sun, illuminating the edges of silhouetted mountains, making them look less like formations of rock and earth, and more like some kind of massive crystal shrine. It was a spectacle that only lasted a few seconds, much like an eclipse, while the sun is aligned at the perfect angle to produce a glimmering halo.

The gratitude we had expressed during meditation expanded exponentially, as each of us felt incredibly thankful to not just see, but take part in such an enchanting moment.

I smiled.

Good morning, Machu Picchu.

As if nature itself sought to return my greeting, a condor glided past us with graceful ease.

I recalled that the condor represented the Upper World, or Hanan Pacha, which was the domain of the gods and spirits. It was this creature, the messenger between humans and the divine, that we were now meeting firsthand.

With that, we stood and continued to navigate the mountainside, and were led to an enormous, oval-shaped stone precariously placed as though teetering on the brink of a plunge down the steep slope. Jorge, with a calm certainty, laid across the stone, flat on his back. His head arched back to look into the sweeping valley below from an upside-down perspective. Then, inviting us to do the same. We did as he did, laying down and allowing our heads to hang off the edge so our eyes could take in the startling drop to the land below.

Emulating the condor, we were asked to observe the world as this sacred creature does. It was a surreal experience, seeing the world upside-down, unfettered by the usual bounds of perspective and direction. Once again, as with so many spots on this adventure, a sense of calm engulfed me as I surrendered myself to the completely novel experience and altering my viewpoint to an unfamiliar one.

This moment made me understand the reverence for the condor in Andean cosmology, as a symbol of freedom, vision, and a higher perspective. It was as though we were momentarily granted its divine abilities to rise above earthly limitations and glimpse the world through the eyes of a creature that effortlessly bridges the gap between humans and the gods.

As we embodied the energy of the condor, Jorge reminded us that this was more than a physical exercise, but a spiritual one as well. In their rituals and ceremonies, shamans frequently call upon the spirit of the condor for guidance, wisdom, and protection, just as we were doing in that moment.

By viewing the world through the eyes of the condor, we were not just altering our physical perspective, but our spiritual one as well. With that, I felt as though I had been taken one step closer to understanding the interconnectedness of all realms of existence.

This was the final stop of our trip, and I couldn't help being struck by the depth of the journey I had undertaken. This was more than just a tour through the Andes, so much more than a simple visit to Peru's highlands. It was a spiritual pilgrimage, one that had taken me from the streets of Cusco to the floating islands of Lake Titicaca, and now to the sacred place of Machu Picchu, with every step guided by the wisdom of our wonderful shaman, Jorge.

Much like the preparation for traditional plant medicine ceremonies, where "set"—our intention or mindset—and "setting"—the environment— frame our experiences, my journey through these sacred spaces had been a lesson in the interconnectedness of these two things. It was in these revered locations, amid the splendor of nature and the echoes of ancient civilizations, that I had learned the true meaning of trust, of surrender, and of the limitless potential of the human mind when open to exploration and understanding.

Throughout the journey, my heart had been a vessel for profound emotions—love and gratitude foremost among them, but also respect. Respect for these sacred places that had stood the test of time, for the people who continued to uphold their traditions and heritage, and for our planet, which holds such wonders within its embrace.

Throughout it all, I only came to understand even deeper the transformative power of gratitude. This emotion, more profound than any other, has the ability to alter our perceptions and open our hearts to the vast wonders that surround us.

As I descended from Machu Picchu, ready to return to Cusco and eventually the comforts of home, I took one last look at the peaks. I knew then that this journey was complete. The chapter may be closing, but the experiences I had lived would continue to shape my life.

Ayahuasca

It's been 18 years since my first Ayahuasca experience, and even today, the memory of that initial encounter lingers as an illuminating beacon in my spiritual journey. Back then, Ayahuasca was a mystery to me; a sacred gift offered by a shaman, it promised a voyage into the unknown recesses of spiritual healing and growth.

Ayahuasca has been deeply rooted in the rituals and medicinal practices of the indigenous peoples of the Amazon forest for centuries, a testament to its age-old role in the exploration of the human psyche. Its origins are shrouded by pre-history, and handed down through oral traditions, making it an enigmatic figure in the pantheon of plant-based medicines.

The term "Ayahuasca," derived from the Quechua language of the Andean region, translates to "vine of the soul" or "vine of the spirits." The words "Aya," meaning "soul" or "spirit," and "huasca," translating to "vine" or "rope," harmonize into an embodiment of its transformative potential - a bridge that allows communication with our ancestors and spirits.

While many individuals embark on spiritual quests to the Andean region in pursuit of Ayahuasca ceremonies, my introduction to it came as a pleasant surprise during my first visit to Peru. Our shaman had arranged for a Quechua shaman to prepare the sacred vine and lead us through an authentic ceremony. It was an extraordinary gift that allowed me to partake in a centuries-old tradition within the heart of the Quechua community.

The Quechua people are indigenous to the Andes and have a profound connection with nature and the cosmos. Some members of their community who reside in the Amazon region also incorporate Ayahuasca ceremonies for purposes of healing and spiritual growth. Renowned for their deep-rooted understanding of Ayahuasca as a healing medicine, Quechua shamans bring an authenticity to these ceremonies that's increasingly rare in the face of rising Ayahuasca tourism and commercialization. Therefore, experiencing this sacred brew in such an original context held a particular significance for me.

Seated on cushions laid out on the floor, we formed a circle within a space that radiated a serene ambiance. Sacred objects such as crystals, a condor feather, coca leaves, and an assortment of local flowers adorned a vibrant, traditionally woven textile in the center. The soft glow from a candle illuminated this spiritual array, creating a sense of reverence and anticipation. The shaman, holding a bottle filled with a carefully brewed medicinal concoction of vine and plants, initiated the ceremony with blessings and chants.

We approached the shaman, one by one, to receive our dose from the "vine of the spirits". I accepted the small cup with both hands, brimming with intentions for the journey ahead, before returning to my seat to observe others doing the same. The shaman, attuned to the needs of each individual, distributed different amounts to each person.

As we completed the first round, the shaman began the second part of the ritual, which involved rhythmic singing and drumming in the indigenous language. The melody, acting as a lullaby, pulled us towards a mystical connection with the plant. These soothing sounds echoed in the background, magnifying each sensation and vibration as the medicine worked its way through our bodies.

I felt a growing heaviness inching from my feet upwards, making its presence known in every single cell. The rhythmic drumming seemed to have entered my being, orchestrating a synchronic dance within me. As I allowed myself to sink into this sensation, each cell seemed to buzz with life, creating a powerful energy that moved from the very tip of my toes to the crown of my head.

As this internal symphony of sensations unfolded, my visual and auditory senses expanded, engulfing me in a cascade of unique experiences. Images swirled, blurring and distorting my surroundings as if seen through a psychedelic lens. Candlelights danced erratically, resembling a time-lapse, and the sounds around me amplified, creating an ethereal experience.

While part of me desired to keep my eyes closed to fully immerse myself in these sensations, the curiosity to understand how others were experiencing their journeys tempted me to steal occasional peeks. Some appeared uncomfortable, others purged, while some were simply lost in stillness or restlessness.

The initial experience felt like a release of pent-up pressure, akin to the process of detoxification. It was reminiscent of an abscess's inflammation, a surge of discomfort, tension, and pain that reaches its peak before the purging release. This seemed to be Ayahuasca's initial work on us - a cleanse, a detoxification of both the body and the mind, setting the stage for deeper communication with various realms of consciousness.

Despite the overwhelming physical sensations and a sense of teetering on the edge of a conscious dream, I managed to remain present and calm. Each moment, my body pulsed with the rhythm of this sacred dance between the physical and the spiritual, tension surging and receding through the six to eight-hour process.

Throughout this journey, I observed that our experiences varied greatly, influenced by our unique life experiences, belief systems, attitudes, mindset, and intentions. For some, the process seemed to dredge up deeply imprinted traumas, serving as a form of mental detoxification. For others, it appeared to be a journey of enlightenment, awakening them to a deeper level of existence.

As a first-time consumer of a DMT-rich substance, I was now fully immersed in uncharted territory. However, reflecting on my past experiences—particularly the Darkness Retreat, which had been my first direct brush with DMT—I realized that those three weeks spent in darkness had primed me for this journey.

My familiarity with the sensation of DMT meant I was spared the discomfort often associated with purging or emotional detoxification. Instead, my journey with Ayahuasca felt like a gentle purification process. A mindful clearing and cleaning of my physical and mental spaces took place, coupled with some visual distortions and altered sensory perceptions. It wasn't a disruptive upheaval, but a graceful dance of transformation, guided by the vine of the soul. This ceremonial journey through the realms of consciousness and self-perception was an unparalleled experience that added profound depth to my understanding of personal growth and healing.

The conclusion of the Ayahuasca ceremony signaled a divergence of paths for each participant. While some opted to sleep within the sacred circle of the ceremonial hall, letting the lingering vibrations of the ceremony continue to resonate within them, others, including myself, chose to return to their personal sleeping areas. The subtle hum of the energetic detoxification process carried on within me, reverberating through the night.

It felt as though Ayahuasca was still diligently at work, coursing through my nervous system and energetic pathways, touching every aspect of my physical body. Even now, I wonder if this experience was the vine of the soul's mechanism for rewiring and repairing me.

The dawn of the next morning always brought an astonishing sense of clarity and lightness. My mind felt unburdened, my heart swelled with an abundance of love, and an intense feeling of openness and loving kindness radiated from me. It was an immensely beautiful and meaningful experience, adding a new dimension to my understanding of existence.

Reflecting on my initial encounter with Ayahuasca, I am struck by the intrigue and curiosity it stirred within me. The profound nature of the experience urged me to seek a deeper understanding of what transpired beneath the surface. How was it that this ancient brew could orchestrate such vivid hallucinations, such transformation of perception, and such profound shifts in self-awareness? What was happening inside my brain as I drank this plant-based concoction? What was the science behind this mystical experience?

I'd like to take some time to answer these questions with you, dear reader, as the workings "behind the curtain" are of equal importance to the experience itself. The science and spirituality form a continuum, each capable of informing the other and therefore creating a deeper understanding of each.

N,N-Dimethyltryptamine, or DMT, is a potent psychedelic compound known to influence the human brain in a variety of ways. The mechanisms and full extent of its effects are yet to be comprehensively understood, but there is substantial evidence pointing to its ability to bind to serotonin receptors, increase brain activity, and even simulate experiences akin to near-death phenomena.

As I mentioned, the traditional Ayahuasca brew is primarily composed of two plants. Their more scientific nomenclature identifies them as banisteriopsis caapi, the vine, and the leaves of the plant called Psychotria viridis, or sometimes other plants that contain DMT. While DMT is capable of inducing profound hallucinogenic experiences, it is generally inactive when ingested orally on its own because an enzyme in our stomachs, monoamine oxidase (MAO), breaks it down swiftly.

Banisteriopsis caapi, however, contains harmala alkaloids, including harmine and harmaline, which act as MAO inhibitors (MAOIs). These substances temporarily disable the MAO enzymes in the body, preventing them from breaking down DMT. So, when brewed together, the MAOIs in the B. caapi vine allow the DMT in the P. viridis leaves to bypass the body's natural defense mechanism and reach the bloodstream and, eventually, the brain. This sophisticated ethno-pharmacological technique is a testament to the profound knowledge possessed by the indigenous cultures who traditionally use Ayahuasca.

DMT's strong affinity for the serotonin (5-HT) receptors in the brain, especially the 5-HT2A receptor, can significantly alter mood, perception, and several other cognitive functions. Research has also indicated that DMT might boost activity and connectivity in certain areas of the brain, contributing to complex visual hallucinations and profound shifts in thought and perspective.

Interestingly, DMT, much like other psychedelics, is suggested to decrease activity in the Default Mode Network (DMN) - a network of interacting brain regions that is active when the mind is at rest. This might be connected to the experiences of ego dissolution reported during psychedelic experiences.

The connections between DMT experiences and near-death experiences (NDEs) are anecdotal yet intriguing, with both involving experiences of transcending the physical body, moving through a tunnel, communicating with other entities, and experiencing profound shifts in perspective.

Indeed, delving deeper into the specific ways that Ayahuasca can significantly impact the mind provides a fascinating perspective on the sheer complexity and variety of experiences that individuals may encounter during their journeys with this sacred brew.

The effects of Ayahuasca can range widely among different individuals, depending on a host of variables. These include factors like the dosage of the brew, the individual's current and past mental and emotional states, as well as the environment or 'setting' during the experience. The 'set' also plays a crucial role in shaping the journey - this refers to the intention, expectation, and mindset of the individual partaking in the ceremony.

Let's take a closer look at the fascinatingly wide spectrum of effects that have been reported by those who have experienced a brush with ayahuasca. They can be broken down into six macro-categories.

1. Altered Perceptions: Consuming Ayahuasca often leads to a significant shift in perception. This can manifest as vivid and intricate visual and auditory hallucinations that could distort one's sense of reality. Some report distortions in their perception of time, with moments feeling like eternity and hours passing in an instant. Others experience a heightened sensitivity to colors and sounds,

leading to a uniquely intensified sensory experience.

2. Emotional Release: Ayahuasca ceremonies often facilitate a strong emotional release. Participants might experience a broad spectrum of emotions ranging from profound euphoria to intense fear, sadness, or anger. This emotional catharsis is frequently linked to the revisitation of past memories or traumas, inviting opportunities for healing and resolution.

3. Insight and Perspective Shifts: Another common report from Ayahuasca users is the gaining of profound insights and significant shifts in their perspective. Many individuals recount seeing situations from their past in a new light or gaining a deepened understanding of themselves, others, and the world around them. This newfound wisdom often leads to changes in personal values and beliefs, altering their perception of life and their place in it.

4. Ego Dissolution: Ayahuasca, like many other psychedelic substances, can induce a state of 'ego dissolution.' This is characterized by a loss or disintegration of the personal identity or 'self.' This often leads to feelings of unity or interconnectedness with others, nature, and the universe at large - an experience that many find profoundly transformative and spiritually enriching.

5. Mystical Experiences: Many people report having profound spiritual or mystical experiences under the influence of Ayahuasca. These experiences can include feelings of transcending the physical body, communicating with higher powers or spiritual beings, and even

traversing other realms or dimensions. Such encounters, often deeply personal and profound, can shape and redefine one's spiritual understanding and beliefs.

6. Therapeutic Effects: Preliminary research has suggested that Ayahuasca may also have potential therapeutic effects. This includes reducing symptoms of depression, anxiety, PTSD, and addiction. Participants often recount a sense of cleansing or healing following the Ayahuasca experience. However, these effects and the mechanisms behind them are not fully understood, warranting more comprehensive research and investigation.

The effects of Ayahuasca, therefore, are multidimensional and deeply personal, offering a unique journey into the self, accompanied by a broad range of perceptual, emotional, cognitive, and spiritual transformations.

In today's world, Ayahuasca is sought after for two primary reasons—recreational enjoyment and personal growth. Recreational users are often intrigued by Ayahuasca's ability to induce intense visual hallucinations and altered states of consciousness.

Despite the profound experiences it can provide, recreational use is potentially risky, mainly when devoid of proper support, supervision, or understanding of the psychological and physical effects of Ayahuasca. Moreover, using this sacred vine as a form of recreation can be viewed as a slight to the Indigenous cultures that revere it.

On the other hand, those who consume Ayahuasca for

personal growth and self-exploration approach the plant with a clear intention. The exploration could involve seeking to understand and heal from past traumas, gain insights into personal behavior, relationships, or to explore spiritual or existential questions. This approach, usually conducted in a ceremonial context under practitioners' supervision, encourages a respectful and mindful engagement with Ayahuasca.

As a practitioner of spiritual healing and growth, it's important to note that Ayahuasca ceremonies should be conducted properly and respectfully. This sacred practice deserves reverence and acknowledgment for the traditional and ancient wisdom it represents. In a world where psychedelic medicine and psychedelic-assisted therapies are re-emerging, it's important to remember that not everyone is suited to seek out these experiences. For those committed to personal growth and self-discovery, the exploration of Ayahuasca may be beneficial. However, it's crucial to keep in mind the importance of the set and setting, and to be aware of your expectations, intentions, environment, and companions.

With the rise of Ayahuasca tourism, it's critical to conduct thorough research before participating in these sacred ceremonies. In this pursuit, remember—those who genuinely seek will undoubtedly find the setting and the guidance that best aligns with their journey.

Authenticity, respect, and care are paramount.

Over the course of several years, from 2005 to 2012, my relationship with Ayahuasca deepened. With every annual ceremony, my understanding of myself, my surroundings, and the intricate web of life unfurled a bit more. Each journey presented its unique palette of experiences and insights, progressively shedding light on the path ahead.

In some ceremonies, my consciousness would dance with resplendent, colorful snake patterns that filled my visual field—a common motif reported by many Ayahuasca users. Other times, I found myself held in the loving arms of blissful stillness, a profound quietude that whispered secrets of existence in silent syllables. By the last ceremony in this seven-year period, I was cradled in an overwhelming sense of openness, unconditional love, and spontaneous joy. I felt a timeless sense of contentment and happiness that didn't beg for reason or explanation.

It simply *was*.

The last Ayahuasca session I attended took place in the year 2012. This final rendezvous with the 'vine of souls' felt complete, as if all the lessons that needed to be imparted had been revealed. I'd learned the value of balance—that fulfillment required neither excessive indulgence nor accepting inadequacy. The ceremony, like the years that had preceded it, was perfect in its own unique way.

This felt as though it was not simply the perfect way, but the perfect time, to conclude my exploration of Ayahuasca. After all, I was standing on the brink of what had become a fairly mainstream prophecy—the conclusion of the mayan calendar.

Although I can't say I ever bought into the theory of the apocalypse choosing to strike in the year 2012, I did always believe it would be a time of transformation. It is that transformation—both practical and mystical—that I would like to explore with you next.

Dharamsala

The spring of 2008 marked my inaugural voyage to Dharamsala, fueled by a desire to explore the realm of traditional Indian medicine, often known as Ayurvedic Medicine. Derived from the Sanskrit words "Ayur," meaning life, and "Veda," meaning science or knowledge, "Ayurveda" can be translated as the "science of life." This holistic health system doesn't merely concern itself with physical well-being; it interweaves the mental, emotional, and spiritual facets of wellness into its healing approach, rooted deeply in the ancient philosophies of India. My focal point for this particular journey was a detoxifying and rejuvenating Ayurvedic process known as "Panchakarma."

Accompanied by a group led by a cherished friend, an internationally acclaimed qigong instructor, author, and researcher, our adventure began in Delhi. From there, we embarked on a 12-hour bus ride across India's rural terrains.

Located in the scenic Indian state of Himachal Pradesh, Dharamsala holds an intricate tapestry of history and spiritual significance. Long before its transformation into a hub of Tibetan culture and spirituality, Dharamsala was prized for its breathtaking beauty, lush tea gardens, and its appeal to nature enthusiasts. During the colonial era, it served as a favored summer retreat, its enchanting landscape offering a welcome respite from the summer heat.

However, the narrative of Dharamsala took an extraordinary turn after 1959. Following the Tibetan uprising, His Holiness the Dalai Lama sought refuge from Tibet and was graciously offered sanctuary in Dharamsala by the Indian government. This marked the beginning of a significant metamorphosis for this picturesque city, as it became the headquarters of the Tibetan government-in-exile and the home of the Dalai Lama himself.

In the wake of the Dalai Lama's arrival, Dharamsala witnessed a large influx of Tibetans fleeing from their homeland, a poignant exodus that eventually led to the formation of what is now often called the "Tibetan refugee village" or "Little Lhasa." This vibrant settlement, more formally recognized as the "Tibetan Exile Community" or "Tibetan Colony," is duly acknowledged by the Indian government as a refugee settlement.

Today, Dharamsala is more than a mere refugee settlement—it stands as a living testament to the resilience of the Tibetan people and their steadfast commitment to preserving their unique cultural heritage. Its streets are lined with monasteries, temples, schools, and cultural institutions that dutifully safeguard and nurture Tibetan culture and identity. Its inhabitants, bound by their shared history and cultural identity, continue to contribute to this community, working in businesses that highlight their vibrant culture. From the sale of traditional Tibetan handicrafts and medicine to the serving of authentic Tibetan food, each corner of Dharamsala echoes with an extraordinary blend of historical significance, cultural richness, and enduring spiritual devotion.

Our group, having weathered the journey, arrived in Dharamsala as morning light started to spread across the city. As I stepped off the bus, the sense of anticipation was palpable. The long ride had been a minor detour, and the real journey was just beginning.

Upon our arrival in Dharamsala, we were set to dive deep into the practice of "Panchakarma," a central component of Ayurvedic medicine. The term "Panchakarma" stems from two roots: "Pancha," meaning "five" in my native language, which has evolved from Pali and Sanskrit, and "Karma," often understood as the principle of cause and effect in various traditions. In Buddhism, 'karma' is also interpreted as the "cycle of rebirth."

In the sphere of Ayurvedic treatments, the concept of Panchakarma holds substantial significance, representing a powerful therapeutic process. It emphasizes the crucial role of detoxification and rejuvenation as key elements in maintaining and restoring health. This procedure is designed to cleanse the body of toxins, helping to restore harmony and balance.

The Panchakarma process is meticulously structured, usually starting with a preparatory phase. This includes

internal and external oleation—where specific oils are used
—and induced sweating, which aids in the mobilization of
toxins, guiding them towards the digestive tract. After this
preparation, the main procedures follow, engineered to
thoroughly eliminate these loosened toxins from the body.

The entire process is carefully bookended with a post-
treatment care phase. This encompasses dietary
regulations, the necessity of adequate rest, and
rejuvenation practices—all designed to solidify and extend
the benefits of the treatment. The intention was not just to
cleanse, but to rejuvenate, restoring vitality and inner
harmony. As I embarked on this journey, I was prepared
for the transformation that lay ahead.

For the next three weeks, our days in Dharamsala took
on a rhythm of their own. Each day began and concluded
with the harmonious cadence of qigong movement
practices, the artful dance of energy and meditation
creating an undercurrent of tranquility amid our rigorous
regimen.

Throughout the day, we were individually scheduled to
consult with a local team of Ayurvedic physicians
specializing in Panchakarma. In private sessions, they
examined each of us, tailoring the treatment protocols to
our specific needs. The range of treatments varied
significantly. Some were more intensive than others,
involving a blend of prescribed medicines, herbs, specific
food regimens, and schedules for enemas.

These treatments embarked us on a path of intense
cleansing. Some of us faced purging from both ends -
vomiting induced to cleanse the upper digestive system,

and laxatives administered to cleanse the lower intestines. The experience of induced vomiting, though aimed at cleansing the upper digestive system, was widely regarded as the most uncomfortable. Enemas, on the other hand, considered the mildest of the treatments, were favored by many. We found a way to jest amidst the rigors of our treatments, our camaraderie fueled by shared experiences and the understanding that this process was in service of our holistic health.

I found myself among the fortunate few with a prescribed treatment protocol that was mild, requiring only occasional enemas and massage. Despite the variety of experiences, each of us was united by a single purpose —to embrace the rejuvenating potential of Panchakarma. Our shared journey, an intricate dance of physical resilience and spiritual depth, was a testament to our commitment to health and well-being.

As I reflect on the experiences of my journey in Dharamsala, I find intriguing parallels between the tenets of Ayurveda and Tibetan medicine, and my current work with psychedelic studies. Despite their disparate historical and cultural contexts, traditional Indian medicine (Ayurveda), Tibetan medicine (Sowa Rigpa), and the use of psychoactive plants in various healing traditions converge on shared foundational principles and objectives. Each system perceives the profound interconnectedness of our physical, psychological, mental, and spiritual health. Each employs distinctive strategies to engender balance and wellness, often pivoting on some form of detoxification.

Ayurveda illustrates the detoxification principle through

the Panchakarma therapy. This age-old process, steeped in ritual and discipline, strives to cleanse the body of toxins and restore the balance of the three doshas (Vata, Pitta, Kapha). Similarly, Sowa Rigpa employs a therapeutic technique known as 'Nadisodhana', a purification therapy designed to purge the body of detrimental elements to maintain equilibrium among the three "nyepas" (Lung, Tripa, Beken).

Sowa Rigpa is deeply embedded within the Tibetan way of life, with its principles echoing down the ages, reaching back to pre-Buddhist times, to the native "Bon" tradition in Tibet. This makes it an ancient art form, one that has been practiced and perfected over 2,500 years.

This method of healing represents a comprehensive approach to healing, expertly blending elements of spiritual, behavioral, and physical therapies. It is more than a medical practice; it's an integrated, unified art form. Sowa Rigpa conceptualizes illness not as a solitary, independent event, but as a manifestation of an evolving disequilibrium among various psychosomatic and cosmophysical elements. This dynamic imbalance has roots that can be traced back to two distinct levels: the primordial, emerging from cosmic forces, and the immediate, expressed in the tangible physical body.

There's a common distinction drawn between "Western versus Eastern Medicine." In many cases, a person will sternly declare that they "believe in" one and not the other —either criticizing the West while praising the East, or dismissing the East while empowering the West. Personally, I believe this mindset to be one that only results in a net-loss of well-being. Still, it is important to explore the distinctions that can be drawn between the two styles of medicine.

In stark contrast to Eastern Medicine, the Western school of medicine, with its foundational base in the biomedical sciences, tends to focus primarily on the physical facets of health. Within the Western perspective, diseases are predominantly observed and interpreted through the prism of anatomical, physiological, and biochemical processes.

The diagnostics approach in Sowa Rigpa is equally distinctive, with Tibetan medicine practitioners relying on an assortment of unique techniques. These include pulse reading, urine analysis, and detailed examination of a patient's tongue, eyes, skin, and physical behaviors. Meanwhile, Western medicine uses an array of modern diagnostic tools, from laboratory tests and imaging technologies to physical examinations, to diagnose diseases. Observing these two healthcare systems, each shaped by unique cultural and historical influences, approaches the concept of disease and wellness in such divergent ways is something that will forever-fascinate me.

Be it Sowa Rigpa, Ayurveda, Amazonian Shamanism, or some other indigenous healing practice, acts of purging our purification have a role to play, and this is often achieved by harnessing the power of psychoactive plants and psychedelic compounds.

Employed within the framework of ritual or ceremony,

these substances facilitate emotional, psychological, and spiritual cleansing. Some psychoactive substances are believed to enable individuals to confront and 'purge' psychological traumas, akin to a form of psycho-spiritual detoxification.

Beyond detoxification, a shared precept among these practices is the emphasis on holistic health and interconnectedness. In both Ayurveda and Sowa Rigpa, health is not solely defined by the absence of disease. Instead, it represents a state of balanced existence that encompasses physical, mental, and spiritual wellness. In a similar vein, the use of psychoactive plants and psychedelic compounds often seeks to foster a sense of connectedness—to oneself, others, and the world.

In the aftermath of my journey, these commonalities stood starkly against the backdrop of my experiences, combining seemingly individual stroke of a brush on a canvas into a large and beautiful painting. The resonance of these teachings—rooted in different cultures, yet converging on shared truths—left an indelible mark on my perspective, infusing my work and life with a deeper appreciation for the multifaceted nature of health and healing.

The Dalai Lama

The first time I met His Holiness, the Dalai Lama, was an unforgettable moment, a turning point etched vividly in my memory. It was during his visit to Emory University in 2010 where I was involved in the Compassion-Based Cognitive Therapy (CBCT) program, a significant part of the Emory-Tibet Science Initiative.

His Holiness, the 14th Dalai Lama, Tenzin Gyatso, was visiting Emory University to offer private teachings to students and community members. At the time, I was residing in Atlanta, Georgia, and considered myself incredibly fortunate to be part of a small group in the university lecture hall, listening to his teachings live for the first time. His presence was palpable, his words profound, and the experience was beyond any classroom learning.

This program explored the potential of loving-kindness and compassion as mechanisms to manage stress and anxiety and to counteract burnout. It was an exquisite confluence of spirituality and science, offering a transformative perspective on emotional health and well-being.

The practice of loving-kindness and compassion, a cornerstone of His Holiness's teachings, was explored in-depth through our work in the CBCT program. It was both humbling and enlightening to discover that these fundamental principles of compassion could lead individuals to novel states of mind. A burgeoning body of neuroscientific research supports this, demonstrating that such practices can significantly impact brain wave patterns, consciousness, and neurological pathways.

Over the coming years, I would have the opportunity to learn under His Holiness on multiple occasions at Emory University: in 2010, 2012, and 2013. These experiences were further enriched when I visited him in Dharamsala and Bodhgaya. Each encounter deepened my understanding of the interconnectedness of the human experience, of the universality of compassion and kindness, and of the potential within each of us to transform our minds and lives.

My impressions of His Holiness the Dalai Lama started long before our first in-person meeting. I had been an avid collector of his books and had developed a deep admiration for his wisdom. But nothing could truly prepare me for our initial encounter. The Dalai Lama radiated an aura of warmth and authenticity that immediately put everyone at ease. His infectious sense of humor added an unexpected touch of relatability to his spiritual persona.

As I interacted with him more frequently over the years and deepened my exploration of Tibetan practices, I came to recognize and appreciate the sharpness of his intellect and the intensity of his focus. Despite his considerable age, his memory was astounding, his spirit indefatigable.

Yet, my interactions with him went beyond just admiration and reverence. They were deeply transformative experiences. His wisdom, particularly in the realm of spirituality seemed to reach far beyond what he expressed in his teachings to the public. I realized that to truly understand and experience such profound wisdom and inner peace, one had to undertake a personal journey of self-discovery. It was not something that could be taught; it was something that had to be experienced.

His Holiness was a warrior of peace, his soul enlightened, his demeanor emanating loving-kindness and compassion. This image of him, this understanding, is what has stayed with me over the years. It is a testament to the profound impact a single person can have on others, especially when that person is as spiritually profound and authentic as His Holiness the Dalai Lama.

The teachings of the Dalai Lama extend far beyond the domain of religious doctrines. They serve as a universal guide to attaining mental wellbeing, promoting attributes such as self-awareness, empathy, and compassion, which are quintessential elements of a balanced mind. His wisdom shines light on tools such as mindfulness and meditation, practices that have been scientifically shown to combat stress, anxiety, and depression.

Mindfulness, as His Holiness often elucidates, involves being entirely present, immersing oneself in the experience of the moment, free from distraction or judgment.

Meditation provides a method to cultivate this state of tranquil awareness, facilitating a deep connection with one's internal processes, by leading to a clearer and more focused mind.

Furthermore, the Dalai Lama's teachings emphasize the fundamental interconnectedness of all beings. By urging individuals to look beyond their personal concerns, he advocates for the expansion of consciousness. Such a broadened perspective cultivates empathy, mitigates egocentric thinking, and nurtures a sense of belonging. It opens the way for recognizing our inherent connection with all of existence, contributing to a healthier mental state and an elevated consciousness.

His Holiness underscores the importance of inner peace as the groundwork for outer peace, the peace that manifests in our society. He argues that the tranquility we cultivate within ourselves ultimately radiates outward, shaping a more harmonious world. This external peace is but a reflection of our internal serenity. Thus, he is globally recognized as an ambassador of peace, compassion, and tolerance, with his teachings influencing mental health and consciousness at a universal level.

Perhaps one of the most profound aspects of the Dalai Lama's wisdom is its accessibility. His teachings, while rooted in Buddhist philosophy, transcend religious boundaries. They offer insights that can benefit all, irrespective of their faith. They support the dissolution of ego, facilitating the emergence of a state of consciousness that is beneficial for all, a state characterized by clarity, tranquility, and a sense of deep interconnectedness. The profound impact of the Dalai Lama's teachings thus lies not just in their spiritual depth but also in their universal applicability.

Bodhichita, a central concept in Mahayana Buddhism, remains a core element in the Dalai Lama's recent teachings. Often translated as the "mind of enlightenment" or "awakening mind," Bodhichita represents a mindset characterized by a spontaneous desire to attain enlightenment. This desire is fueled by great compassion or 'Maha Karuna' for all sentient beings, a boundless compassion that makes no distinctions. It encompasses the aspiration to achieve enlightenment not merely for oneself but for the benefit of others.

The Dalai Lama's practice of the six perfections— generosity, morality, patience, effort, concentration, and wisdom—serves as the stepping stones on the path to cultivating a Bodhichita mindset. Though these qualities may seem simple or 'ordinary,' their power lies in their ability to transform our lives when lived in each moment, in an 'ordinary' state of mind.

At risk of being redundant, I'm going to repeat these six perfections, only because I believe they can be the mortar in the sturdy structure of a fulfilling life:

Generosity.

Morality.

Patience.

Effort.

Concentration.

Wisdom.

With that re-said, let's get back to it.

Bodhichita is imbued with the practice of the six perfections, serving as a guiding principle towards spiritual awakening.

However, Bodhichita's culmination lies beyond these 'ordinary' practices. An advanced or absolute level of Bodhichita leads to the direct and non-conceptual perception of 'emptiness' or the ultimate nature of reality. This level of enlightenment is achieved through deep meditative practices or from a non-ordinary state of mind.

Thus, Bodhichita encapsulates the essence of the Dalai Lama's teachings—compassion, enlightenment, and the interconnectedness of all beings. It provides a path for spiritual growth that is universally accessible, profoundly transformative, and deeply aligned with the principles of interconnectedness and compassion that His Holiness so passionately advocates.

Bohd Gaya

Having been raised in a household that embraced both Buddhism and Catholicism, I found myself often drawn to the calming echoes of Buddhist chants reverberating from the temples in my home country. My relationship with Buddhism didn't end there. During my college years, I found myself leading the Student Buddhist Society at my university, my enthusiasm for the teachings only intensifying with each passing year.

After I relocated to the U.S. in the mid-1980s, my exploration of Zen Buddhism, the ornate intricacies of Tibetan Buddhism, and numerous other belief systems and religions continued to flourish. Each was unique, yet they all traced back to shared roots of thought. This ability to perceive the shared essence beneath the religious labels felt like unwrapping an invaluable gift life had presented me.

Fast forward to 2022, a whirlwind of fortune swept me off to Bodh Gaya to participate in an enlightening event - a teaching by His Holiness the Dalai Lama and the inauguration of a union of all Buddhist denominations. Bodh Gaya, nestled in the Indian state of Bihar, is more than just a location; it's a beacon for Buddhists worldwide. Revered as the birthplace of Enlightenment, it's said to be the very spot where Siddhartha Gautama, later known as Buddha, first embraced enlightenment in the 5th century BCE.

As I sat beneath the tree, believed to be the very one that sheltered Buddha during his journey to enlightenment, I was overcome with an array of profound emotions. Every day, Bodh Gaya was a hive of activity, with hundreds of thousands of individuals gathering to meditate on the dirt floor of the teaching ground. Regardless of the different practices among Buddhist disciplines, meditation and contemplation unified us all, serving as a universal language—the language of the mind.

It was a beautiful sight to behold. People from every corner of the world, with a symphony of over 30 languages echoing through the air, all gathered to celebrate life and embark on their personal growth. Whether they were there to cultivate loving compassion, in pursuit of truth and the meaning of life, or desperately seeking healing, each individual had their unique motivations. The temple grounds hummed with the resonance of chants, prayers, and the exchange of blessings. It was a moment of unforgettable significance, yet another milestone in my life's journey.

While in Bodh Gaya, I came to realize an intriguing aspect of our consciousness, a phenomenon that is universal yet experienced uniquely by each individual. It is the state of non-ordinary consciousness, which aligns with the theta brainwave state.

No matter where we are or what culture we come from, we all have the potential to enter these non-ordinary states of consciousness. This might be triggered through various methods such as meditation, deep prayer, or the use of certain psychoactive plants. Yet, Tibetans have their unique way of facilitating this transition through their potent rhythmic chanting and rigorous disciplines.

Tibetan chanting serves as a powerful vehicle that can transport us to this distinctive state of mind. It resonates at a frequency that seems to open a gateway to these deeper layers of consciousness. Alongside chanting, practices in Tibetan medicine require mental, visual, and postural focus, such as the complex hand gestures known as mudras. This state of hyperfocus, when the mind is so deeply concentrated that it begins to transcend the immediate physical reality, allows for access to these non-ordinary states. In some advanced Tibetan practices, certain psychoactive plants are used as tools to further facilitate reaching into these profound mental states.

Experiences within this non-ordinary state can greatly differ from person to person. It may feel akin to deep meditation, where one loses their sense of self or perceives a dissolution of their physical body, merging with the space around them. Some describe it as a sensation of becoming one with the universe, floating in space as a speck of dust. It can feel as though we have transcended our physical form and have become nothingness.

In essence, Tibetan practices provide an intriguing approach to consciousness and non-ordinary states of mind, offering unique pathways to explore and understand the profound depths of our being. It was a deep dive into the mystery of consciousness, where I was able to explore and experience the depths of my own mind. This journey was not just about traversing physical landscapes, but also about traversing the inner landscapes of my consciousness.

My time in Bodh Gaya illuminated not a deeper understanding of Buddhism, or any particular practice, but rather the profound power of "faith." As I observed people from all corners of the globe, each carrying their own unique beliefs, converging on this remote place, I was deeply moved. They had journeyed far, stepped out of their comfort zones, and dedicated months of their lives to learning and contemplation in this sacred place. It was a testament to the force of faith, a force strong enough to bridge gaps between nations, languages, and cultures. *faith*

The image of hundreds of thousands of individuals, their collective silence a resonant chorus in itself, was a sight to behold. Yet, when stirred, they could become a roaring sea of gratitude and joy, a demonstration of unity and shared purpose that was as awe-inspiring as it was humbling.

My experiences in Bodh Gaya led me to appreciate the universal nature of faith, a concept imbued with deep and varied meanings across different contexts. At its core, faith could be described as complete trust, confidence, or reliance on someone or something. It often implies a strong belief, requiring no empirical evidence or proof.

Witnessing faith in its many forms, seeing its transformative power at work, I realized that it is indeed one of the most potent forces in the universe. Whether it takes the shape of religious belief, confidence in a healing process, or trust in the potential of the human spirit, faith stands as a universal phenomenon. This realization was, in essence, the most profound lesson of my journey to Bodh Gaya, and it continues to shape my understanding and approach to life.

Camino de Santiago

Not all inspired actions need to come from our inner reservoir of wisdom, whispers in the wind, or deep contemplation. The purveyor of that spark can come in many forms and, in this case, my purveyor was Martin Sheen. The first stirrings of my desire to embark on the pilgrimage of Camino de Santiago were sparked by a movie—*The Way to St James*, starring the aforementioned purveyor of spark.

The film provided a vivid tableau of the myriad of human emotions that come to the fore in our everyday lives - joy and sorrow, humor and excitement, a sense of adventure, and an undercurrent of hope, respect, and trust. It was a cinematic journey, overflowing with life lessons, that explored themes of grief and redemption, self-discovery and spiritual awakening.

As I watched the scenes unfold, I was struck by a profound sense of curiosity and inspiration. Life, it seemed, had grown increasingly hectic, leaving me little room to catch my breath. The pilgrimage portrayed in the film offered a unique opportunity to slow down, providing a respite from the relentless pace of daily life.

By the end of the film, I was on the brink of certainty that I was Camino-bound, but I wanted a deeper understanding of the place and its history before commencing such a journey. My knowledge of the area had been cursory prior to viewing the movie, and I knew that roughly ninety minutes of screen time had only scratched the surface of knowledge.

I wanted to know more. What was the true significance of this place that—let's be honest—I was *definitely* about to explore?

The story of the Camino is tied to the apostle Saint James, who, as tradition holds, preached the Gospel in the Iberian Peninsula following Jesus's death and resurrection. His missionary work eventually led him back to Jerusalem, where he faced martyrdom at the hands of King Herod Agrippa in 44 AD, becoming the first apostolic martyr.

His demise, however, only marked the beginning of his legendary tale. His followers carried his body back to Iberia by sea, journeying inland to bury him at a site that is now recognized as Santiago de Compostela. The burial site was lost to memory until the 9th century, when a hermit named Pelayo was guided to the site by a celestial constellation. Bishop Theodemar of the era authenticated the remains as those of St. James, leading to the place being christened "Campus Stellae" or "Field of the Star", which over time evolved into "Compostela".

King Alfonso II of Asturias, upon hearing of this miraculous discovery, became the inaugural pilgrim to the site, marking the genesis of the Camino de Santiago. To honor the apostle, he commanded the construction of a chapel at the site, a humble precursor to the grand Cathedral of Santiago de Compostela that stands today.

Throughout the Middle Ages, the Camino de Santiago emerged as one of the most significant Christian pilgrimages, standing alongside those to Rome and Jerusalem, and attracting pilgrims from every corner of Europe. The journey has indelibly shaped the cultural, social, and economic fabric of the regions it traverses. While its roots are devoutly religious, the Camino today is a beacon for spiritual seekers of various faiths and beliefs, serving as a retreat from modern life and a path toward inner discovery.

My journey on the Camino trail was not a solitary one; I was accompanied by a group of individuals who added to the richness of this experience. A friend of mine, a tour guide by profession, had coordinated this special trip alongside the owner of the VIP Camino tour. There were about ten of us in total, each bringing our unique perspectives and life experiences to this collective pilgrimage.

The travels on the trail would last 14 days, dedicated to walking and soaking up the tranquility, followed by a week devoted to exploring the local art. These three weeks could be compared to my 21 days in the darkness; both experiences promised a slower pace. There were quite a few differences, of course. For instance, this trip would likely not send me floating into the cosmos or strolling across hot coals, but it was the (relatively) nuanced nature of this exploration that had me so intrigued.

Our pilgrimage along the Camino de Santiago began in Portugal's radiant capital, Lisbon. Our first night was spent at the luxurious Pousada de Lisboa, nestled in the heart of the city. The hotel provided spectacular views of the bustling Terreiro do Paço Square and the serene Tagus River. From Lisbon, we set out for Porto, the starting point of our pilgrimage, a journey steeped in anticipation and excitement.

As we gathered to take our first steps on this transformative journey, a surge of exhilaration washed over us. The anticipation of the walk was as tangible as the cobblestones beneath our eager feet. To ensure our safety and overall well-being, we were provided with a comprehensive guide that detailed self-care routines, essential rules of the pilgrimage, the expected codes of conduct, and contingency plans for emergencies.

Although we were embarking on this journey as a group, it was emphasized that we were individual pilgrims, each with different walking paces and varying levels of physical stamina. Acknowledging these differences, we established in advance designated meeting points along the route. These checkpoints would serve as reunions, places where we could reconvene after periods of solitary introspection during our walks.

We would be free to explore as lone individuals without fear of being lost. One of the defining elements of the Camino de Santiago is its symbolic yellow arrows, painted unobtrusively along the path. These understated guides would be our silent companions, showing us the way at intersections and turns, helping us navigate the trail when it branched off into different directions. The anticipation of setting off, coupled with the preparations, solidified the reality of our impending journey. We were about to embark on an adventure of a lifetime, filled with self-discovery, camaraderie, and spiritual growth.

It was June, which meant right from the first steps of our journey, we were greeted by the kind of weather that travelers dream of. The climate was akin to that of southern California, with temperatures hovering pleasantly between 60 and 70 degrees Fahrenheit, perfect conditions for long walks through unfamiliar terrain.

Our pilgrimage through Portugal was made more comfortable by the assistance of a small vehicle, endearingly dubbed the "Pop Van," for its luxurious nature. This modern Mercedes Benz pop-up van became an integral part of our journey. It relieved us of the strain of carrying heavy belongings, providing safe storage for our supplies and personal items. Each day, the van transported us to our night-time accommodations and, come morning, would deposit us back on the Camino. This kind blend of traditional pilgrimage with the conveniences of contemporary technology allowed us to concentrate on the spiritual and personal aspects of our journey, echoing the "set and setting" concepts essential in psychedelic retreats.

Our route through Portugal was a feast for the senses. The landscape was lush and fertile, teeming with vibrant gardens that burst with aromatic herbs, and an array of enchanting flora and fauna. The path meandered through quaint, charming villages, each with its unique allure, and intermittently opened up to spectacular panoramas of the vast ocean. The richness of the Portuguese stretch, the serene climate, and the convenience provided by the Pop Van, all came together to create a backdrop conducive to self-discovery and surrender, setting the stage for our transformative journey along the Camino de Santiago.

We had one other unique layer of comfort—our choice of sleeping arrangements. Instead of the simpler and more conventional accommodations often preferred by many pilgrims, we chose to stay in paradors. It was a quite agreeable break from the common misinterpretation that all pilgrimages must be punishingly uncomfortable. Though there is certainly merit to a barebones, humble journey, our chosen housing brought an exciting touch of luxury and historical charm to our travels.

The term "parador" originates from the Spanish verb "parar," which translates to "to stop, halt, or stay." Paradors are a chain of Spanish luxury hotels, known as Paradores de Turismo de España, established by the Spanish government in 1928 to boost tourism. Paradors are housed in converted historic buildings. Think: monasteries, castles, or palaces - creating a unique concept in the hospitality industry.

When you stay in a parador, you don't just find rest; you immerse yourself in the echoes of history that pervade the air. Every wall, every corridor is a silent custodian of countless stories that stretch back over centuries. This makes every parador a vessel of heritage and history, and our stay became about much more than just comfortable accommodation. It was like living a fragment of the past, bringing an additional layer of depth to our Camino experience.

Moreover, the paradors' elegance and comfort served as mental nourishment, just as their comfort and safety provided physical sustenance. By creating this balance, we formed an environment that allowed our spirits to express themselves most optimally. As we retired each night to our paradors after a day of walking, we found ourselves ensconced not just in the comfort of luxury but also in the fascinating mosaic of Spanish history.

The Camino de Santiago is more than just a pathway through beautiful landscapes; it's a conduit for entering non-ordinary states of mind. This ties closely to the broader themes of our exploration - the navigation of alternate mental landscapes and the awakening of deeper self-awareness.

Being on a pilgrimage like the Camino involves long periods of solitude and tranquility, an ideal setting for the practice of mindfulness. It invites pilgrims to be fully present in the moment, to perceive each breath, step, and heartbeat without judgment. This immersion in the present can induce a sense of peace, clarity, and a unique viewpoint on our thoughts and emotions.

The repetitiveness of walking, especially within the serenity of nature, can cultivate a meditative state. Much like the rhythmic pulsing of a drum or the chant of a mantra, each footfall becomes a metronome grounding us in the here and now. Meditation, in its various forms, is recognized for its ability to transform our consciousness, leading to heightened self-awareness, increased focus, and deeper relaxation.

As we ventured further north to Santiago de Compostela, we were met with a noticeable drop in temperature, making the air crisp and the atmosphere more bracing. Being enveloped by the grandeur of nature itself is a profound experience. It alleviates stress, boosts happiness, and stimulates cognitive function. The sense of oneness many people experience with the natural world prompts shifts in perspective and fresh insights.

Moreover, the physical exertion inherent in the long walks can trigger the release of endorphins, our body's natural mood enhancers and pain relievers. This surge of "feel-good" chemicals contributes to an overall state of euphoria and well-being.

Walking the Camino also invites deep introspection. Removed from the humdrum routine of everyday life, the journey offers ample opportunity to challenge and question long-held beliefs and thought patterns. This reflective process can lead to significant shifts in perspective, nudging us towards profound personal transformation.

The Camino de Santiago, imbued with centuries of spiritual and religious significance, fosters a connection to something much larger than the self. The humble act of retracing the steps of countless pilgrims over the centuries resonates with a sense of continuity and communal spirit. It whispers of a timeless bond with all those who have sought solace, healing, or answers on the same path.

Accessing new states of consciousness is an intensely personal journey. It requires surrendering to the full potential of our being, shedding preconceived notions, and making room for novel perspectives. Walking the Camino encourages such surrender. As we tread each mile, we open ourselves up to self-understanding and a more nuanced perception of the world around us. On the Camino, we not only traverse physical distance but also the fascinating landscape of the mind.

On the Camino, one becomes part of an ancient, symbolic ritual, a sequence of acts each imbued with profound spiritual significance. From the inaugural step to the placement of a stone at Cruz de Ferro, and finally the cathartic burning of clothes at Finisterre - each of these traditions potentially paves the way towards mystical experiences.

I relinquished the convenience of modern maps and navigational aids, instead trusting the time-honored guidance of yellow arrows marked on stones. This practice demanded a deep sense of trust in the journey, mindfulness about my direction, and heightened awareness of my surroundings. It was as if I was divesting myself of the unnecessary clutter, both mental and physical, to delve into the very core of my being.

The Camino offered a return to simplicity, focusing on basic human needs—sustenance, hydration, and rest. This stripping away of contemporary complexities encouraged a deeper connection to my spiritual essence. The solitude it granted, coupled with the physically demanding nature of the pilgrimage and the sensory immersion in nature, nudged me towards a different state of consciousness, often providing glimpses into spiritual truths.

The rhythm of walking, each footfall resonating like a heartbeat, served to calm my mind, creating a soothing cadence that opened doors to deeper spiritual dimensions. This was not an escape from reality but a deeper dive into it, a journey not just through the picturesque landscapes of Spain, but also through the uncharted terrains of the human psyche.

Along the way, countless churches, chapels, and crosses punctuated the path, beckoning me to pause, to reflect, and to commune with the divine. Each stop was an invitation to introspection, an opportunity to delve into the depths of my own spirituality, breaking the barriers of the ordinary and venturing into the extraordinary realms of the mind.

For many people, the rhythm of life is dictated by a cycle of waking and sleeping, interspersed with work, nourishment, and rest. These patterns become so ingrained that we scarcely consider them, our weekdays distinct from our weekends, our lives arranged neatly around societal norms and expectations. But while on the Camino, our habitual rhythms began to change. Our only task each day was to move forward, to journey on an unfamiliar path, trusting in the arrows that guided our way.

In this new rhythm, I traded my daily routine for a journey into the uncharted depths of my mind, the environment around me, and the fluctuating landscape of my emotions and perceptions. As I traversed the ancient paths, I shed my usual responsibilities and embraced the privilege of self-exploration and spiritual insight. The trail offered a spiritual buffet—a series of rituals, symbols, and elements of nature for me to respect, learn from, and be transformed by.

Walking for hours each day was a novel experience, a departure from my usual activities. This drastic shift led to common challenges like blisters, a token from the Camino reminding me of my journey into the unknown. But with a conscious routine of regular foot checks, sock changes, and careful hydration and nourishment, I kept these discomforts at bay. Each step was a lesson, teaching me resilience, preparation, and self-care.

These 21 days, indeed, were akin to the 21 days I had spent in darkness. But here, the darkness was punctuated by light, by exploration, by the change of night to day, and the constant interplay of my inner and outer worlds. I stepped out of the everyday, entering a space where the ordinary mingled with the extraordinary.

The Camino's rhythm had a transformative effect. It induced clarity, invigorated my creativity, inspired courage, and reaffirmed my existence. It was akin to the psychedelic state of mind, a journey not only of distance but of consciousness—a rhythmic dance through light and dark, known and unknown, the self and the universe, dancing to the timeless beat of the Camino.

Every day on the Camino began and ended with a sense of unity. Our small group gathered each morning over a delicious breakfast, sharing anticipation and excitement for the day's journey ahead. Once the walking concluded and the sun had run its course through the sky, the cycle would culminate in an exquisite dinner, a feast celebrating our achievements, shared experiences, and the endurance of our group spirit.

During the day, we often found ourselves spread out along the trail, walking at our own pace. This dispersion gave way to hours of solitude, enabling us to immerse ourselves in deep thought and introspection. We walked in harmony with the rhythm of nature, a beautiful symphony of sights, sounds, and sensations that invited us to further explore our inner selves.

As we journeyed along, we were never entirely alone. We frequently encountered other pilgrims, each drawn to the Camino for their own reasons, each with their own tale to tell. These meetings became portals into other lives, reminding us of our interconnectedness even in solitude. Conversations, ranging from casual chatter to profound exchanges, created a tapestry of shared experiences, reinforcing the concept of microcosm and macrocosm. Each of us, with our unique journeys, was part of a larger, collective pilgrimage.

Amid the quiet contemplation and deep introspection, we also savored the joy of exploration. Each village we stopped in became an oasis of culture and cuisine, offering delightful local snacks and rejuvenating coffee. These rest stops, although brief, enriched our journey, interweaving our solitary exploration with shared enjoyment, and reminding us that the Camino, like life, is a dance between connection and solitude.

As our pilgrimage continued, we found ourselves resting each night in a variety of locations, each with its unique charm and character. But a few stand-outs not only offered a place for rest but also intertwined with history and culture that left a lasting impression on our memories of the Camino.

One of the gems along the Camino route was the historic Parador de Pontevedra. Nestled in the heart of Pontevedra city, this former palace resonates with elegance and royal grandeur. Walking its corridors, we couldn't help but feel the echos of the past—a sense of nobility, history, and heritage that pervaded every stone and every piece of antique furniture.

Then, we found ourselves at Caldas de Reis, where we spent the night at Torre do Rio. This rural hotel is set in a restored 18th-century mill, nestled amid the stunning Galician landscape. Its unique architecture and serene environment infused a sense of tranquility into our journey, a welcomed contrast to our physically demanding walk. The gentle murmur of the nearby river served as a lullaby, lulling us to a restful sleep and readying us for the next leg of our journey.

As I traversed the diverse terrains of the Camino, I found myself immersed in the embrace of nature. Each step I took, each sight I beheld, led me deeper into an intimate connection with the environment, renewing my sense of awe and reverence for the natural world.

Gardens teeming with life marked my journey, their vibrant blossoms acting as natural milestones. As I walked, I was serenaded by rivers, their rhythmic murmuring a soothing counterpoint to my labored breathing. The babbling of creeks whispered tales of their journey down from the mountains, and the grandeur of bridges – these man-made marvels – lent a sense of gravitas, symbolizing the convergence of nature and human endeavor.

The aviary symphony that accompanied me was a joy to the senses. Birds, in all their magnificent diversity, filled the air with a myriad of songs. Their melodious calls, so unique and yet harmonious, underscored the richness of life on the Camino, turning my journey into a moving concerto of natural sounds.

Occasionally, the path would open up to expansive fields, where the horizon stretched out seemingly to infinity. These open landscapes, dotted with interesting stone formations, inspired contemplation. These monoliths, shaped by millennia of wind and weather, stood as silent witnesses to the passage of time, reminding me of the transient nature of my journey and life itself.

Then, there were times when my path would meander through enchanting groves. Underneath these verdant canopies, I felt as if I were traversing a tranquil forest. The leaf-dappled sunlight filtering down, the crisp scent of earth, and the soothing rustle of foliage created an atmosphere of serenity and deep peace.

In all these ways and more, nature presented itself as an ever-present companion on the Camino, a living, breathing entity that offered me lessons in resilience, harmony, and the transient beauty of existence.

We entered Spain as a unified group, and were greeted by a remarkable transformation in the landscape. The terrain became a collection of majestic mountains, verdant trees, and expansive natural parks. Occasionally, these were punctuated by open areas, their unadorned beauty contrasting with the lush surroundings.

Our path led us through numerous chapels and cathedrals, each holding a fascinating history within their hallowed walls. Nestled within ancient edifices, these sacred spaces were more than mere buildings; they were repositories of faith, testaments to the centuries-old religious traditions that permeate the Camino. Their quiet dignity reminded us of the timeless spiritual quest that has drawn countless souls to this path.

As we moved forward, we encountered an ever-changing tableau of natural and man-made wonders. Dense forests, their canopy whispering stories of nature's cycles, gave way to charming villages, their cobblestone streets narrating the everyday rhythms of local life. Serene farms punctuated the landscape, their simplicity bearing the stamp of a life closely tied to the rhythm of the seasons.

Majestic mountains loomed on the horizon, their peaks seeming to scrape the heavens, an awe-inspiring spectacle of nature's grandeur. I would be remiss if I did not mention the coastal views—breathtaking vistas of the vast sea meeting the sky, the bracing sea air infusing our journey with a sense of expansive freedom.

Above us, the ever-changing sky served as a constant reminder of the passage of time. The shifting hues of dawn, the vibrant blues of midday, the fiery palette of dusk, and the star-studded darkness of night – each phase marked our progress towards our ultimate destination, Santiago de Compostela. As we walked on, each footfall became a step towards understanding the interplay between the tangible journey we were undertaking and the intangible spiritual exploration that was unfolding within us.

Upon entering the Cathedral of Saint James, we wove through a throng of fellow pilgrims, each one shoulder to shoulder in a mass of humanity, all seeking a transformative experience. Our group was overwhelmed with gratitude when we finally stepped inside. Although the pews were filled to capacity, we were surprised to find the front row seats reserved for us. This allowed us the unique privilege of attending a special mass. We sat adjacent to the clergy, immersed in ancient liturgical rhythms and the aromatic scent of frankincense and myrrh, as if transported back through the corridors of time.

Constructed between 1075 and 1211, the cathedral embodies an amalgamation of Romanesque, Gothic, and Baroque architectural styles. Its most revered feature is the Pórtico de la Gloria, a breathtaking Romanesque portico fashioned by Master Mateo and his workshop, under the commission of King Ferdinand II of León.

As I stood in the Cathedral, I found myself consistently reaching this heightened awareness. Sacred spaces have a way of accumulating unique vibrations and frequencies. Upon entering these spaces, one can feel the oscillations of resonant energy patterns, offering experiences akin to psychedelic journeys, yet without any substances involved. It was truly incredible.

I paid my respects to the apostle Saint James the Great at the culmination of my journey in the Cathedral—a moment of deep reverence and reflection that encapsulates the spiritual allure of the Camino de Santiago.

In retrospect, my journey on the Camino was a fertile ground for introspection and self-discovery. With every step on the ancient path, I had unraveled hidden facets of my own self.

Through this pilgrimage, I unearthed a deep-seated passion for walking that had previously lain dormant. I found that walking was more than a vehicle to propel me from one place to another; it was an enriching activity in its own right. It was a dance of the body in harmony with the rhythm of life, an expressive symphony orchestrated by the gentle placing of one foot in front of the other. This movement, tuned to the tempo of nature, allowed me to absorb the beauty of my surroundings in a way I had never experienced before.

Upon my return to the comfort and familiarity of home, I was met with a peculiar sense of longing. My body, having grown accustomed to the ceaseless rhythm of the Camino, pined for the simplistic act of continual motion that had become a cornerstone of my existence during the pilgrimage. This readjustment to my prior routine—once so familiar—now felt jarring and somewhat restrictive.

I longed for a return to the enlightening insights and spiritual nourishment I had tasted on my journey. As I moved forward, integrating this new-found wisdom into my daily life, I discovered that there was no need to physically return to the Camino to regain the soothing spiritual cadence I had come to love so much.

Much like other non-ordinary states of mind, it was something that could be cultivated from within and applied to my surroundings. So, although the pilgrimage is far from me in time and space, the rhythm of the Camino continues to beat within me, echoing its wisdom and serenity long after the physical journey has concluded.

The Golden Triangle

As a child, my life was markedly touched by the profound events that transpired during the turbulent years of 1973 and 1976, most notably the October 6th massacre, in which nearly fifty protestors and demonstrators were killed during a time of extreme political unrest.

At nine years of age, my understanding of the gruesome realities was understandably limited. However, the echoes of instability and unrest—resonating from the conflicts among military officials, civilians, students, and workers—reverberated through my young consciousness.

Thailand, my homeland, was caught in the throes of a political and economic crisis. This period, which many historians refer to as an experiment in democracy, was marred by a state of what could best be described as "chaotic democracy". The details of these political machinations were not my forte. However, from a young age, I gleaned that "politics" encompassed the establishment of rules and agreements. It was about making decisions that dictated how individuals coexisted within a societal framework.

In retrospect, I realize that the turbulence of those years had been deeply embedded within my subconscious. It shaped my perspective and indirectly influenced my choices. So, when I stepped into the realm of higher education, the landscape had subtly shifted for me. Academic achievement, while still important, assumed a secondary role.

Entering university, the primary focus for me and many of my fellow students was no longer merely to accumulate knowledge or aim for stellar grades. The undertones of our pursuits had changed. Many of my generation were now driven by a shared commitment to cultivate love and kindness—towards our fellow beings and our nation that had been through so much.

My understanding of politics, too, evolved during these crucial years. From the sociological perspective I studied, politics emerged not merely as a tool to govern, but also as a means to influence. It represented the ability of individuals or groups to mold the thoughts, actions, and mindsets of people within a nation. The power inherent in this interpretation of politics was both fascinating and daunting.

The political strife of the past and the newfound understanding of politics would play a significant role in shaping my journey. As I delved deeper into my college years, I began volunteering in the Golden Triangle, an endeavor that would test my resilience, challenge my perceptions, and ultimately shape the person I would become.

In the pursuit of higher education, I found my place at Mahidol University, one of the most prestigious institutions in Thailand. It was particularly renowned for its excellence in the field of medicine, distinguishing it from other top-tier universities such as Chulalongkorn, celebrated for its arts and sciences programs, and Thammasat, with its strong focus on political science.

From the moment I set foot on the campus as a freshman, I was absorbed into a culture that emphasized love for others and devotion to humanity. This ethos, woven subtly into every aspect of our university life, took root within me and shaped my approach to the world.

Throughout my college years, I found myself naturally gravitating towards leadership roles within various student organizations. I served as a guiding force in the public health student organization, the medical science student association, and the Buddhism student society. Each of these roles imparted valuable lessons and helped to refine my perspective and approach.

During holidays and school breaks, we transformed our free time into opportunities for meaningful contribution. We initiated and implemented various projects that allowed us to give back to society. From volunteering at free clinics in rural and underserved areas of Thailand to building schools and even toilets in communities that desperately needed them, we strove to make a tangible difference.

One particular focus of our efforts was the development

of infrastructure to provide clean food and water to rural areas and indigenous communities in the Golden Triangle. This region, known more for its illicit opium production than for its living conditions, presented us with a unique set of challenges and rewards. It was here that I witnessed firsthand the resilience of the human spirit, the undeniable strength of community, and the transformative power of love and kindness. Each initiative we undertook further ingrained these values within me, shaping me into a person who believed in the power of active compassion.

As I look back, these college years were not merely about academics or qualifications. They were about understanding humanity, embracing compassion, and making a real difference. They were about recognizing that we all have the capacity to contribute positively to the world around us. In essence, they were about the cultivation of love and kindness—lessons that have remained with me throughout my life.

The Golden Triangle, a term famously coined by the CIA, refers to the area along the northern border of Thailand and its adjacent countries. This region was once known as a major hub for opium cultivation—a history that is deeply complex and entwined with social, political, and economic influences.

Situated within the valleys and slopes of the northern Thai mountains, over 3,000 villages thrived. Known as hill tribes or highlanders, and referred to as Chao Kao in the native Thai language, these ethnic communities were remarkable in their beauty, vibrancy, and skillful way of life.

The roots of opium cultivation in the Golden Triangle can be traced back to the 19th century when the British Empire played a significant role in fostering opium production in neighboring regions under its control, such as India and Burma. To meet China's demand amidst its addiction crisis, the British encouraged opium farming, which eventually spilled into the border regions of what are now Myanmar and Thailand.

By the early 20th century, opium production in the region continued to expand, spurred by economic considerations and a lack of alternative livelihoods for local communities. The remote, mountainous terrain of the Golden Triangle provided ideal conditions for opium poppy cultivation, and soon, it became a prosperous income source for farmers. Ethnic minority groups in the region, including the Akha, Lisu, and Karen, became involved in opium farming as a means of survival.

During the 1960s and 70s, the Golden Triangle emerged as the world's leading opium-producing region, catering to a significant share of the global heroin demand. The flourishing drug trade involved a host of actors—local warlords, corrupt officials, and international criminal networks. The profits from the opium trade exacerbated political and social instability, fueling conflicts and unrest in the region.

However, by the late 20th century, the tide began to turn. International pressure, primarily from the United States, led to intensified counter-narcotics operations and the introduction of alternative development programs. These initiatives aimed to provide opium farmers with alternative livelihoods, a shift from illicit drug production to sustainable agricultural practices. Slowly but steadily, opium cultivation in the Golden Triangle began to recede, giving way to other agricultural practices and economic activities. It was within this transforming landscape that I found my purpose, merging my academic pursuit with a heartfelt mission to uplift and empower these communities.

My initiation into volunteer work, which entailed assisting the indigenous hill tribes of the Golden Triangle and the underserved rural areas of Thailand, began in my college years. I was your typical teenager, driven by a sense of adventure and an insatiable curiosity. Each activity I undertook seemed to come out of an irresistible allure, driven more by instinct and "unseen influences" than by any logical explanation. These steps were, in many ways, my life lessons and continue to fuel my excitement for learning, even now, as I maintain the mindset of a beginner.

During this time, my aunt Pense, a prominent figure in the new-age subculture devoted to helping humanity, served as a key influence and role model. She spent a significant portion of her time exploring the hill tribes of the Golden Triangle and raising funds to support the indigenous people of the region. In this period of my life, her influence was pivotal, steering me towards service and opening my eyes to the pressing needs of these communities.

Our work received financial backing from various non-governmental organizations (NGOs). In one memorable project, I had the opportunity to learn from my aunt and her friend, John. The project took me directly to the communities in the Golden Triangle, where we focused on teaching them about sustainable crop alternatives. Our primary aim was to equip the community with the knowledge and skills necessary to diversify their agricultural practices and enhance their food security.

One of the crops we introduced was wheat. We primarily worked with the Lisu village, instructing them on various aspects of wheat cultivation—from planting and harvesting to processing it into food, such as bread. Our hope was to diminish their reliance on opium cultivation and pave the way for a more sustainable livelihood.

The sight of the community's enthusiasm and willingness to learn and adopt these new agricultural techniques was genuinely heartening. Today, although opium cultivation persists to a degree in the Golden Triangle, the region has made significant strides. It has diversified its economy, transitioning towards legal and sustainable agriculture, tourism, and trade. Governments and international organizations continue to collaborate to address the challenges of drug production and trafficking, focusing on socio-economic development, law enforcement, and drug rehabilitation programs.

The lessons learned from these early volunteer experiences have continued to shape my perspective and inform my actions. The sense of fulfillment derived from serving others and contributing positively to society still motivates me today. Every moment, every interaction, every project has been an integral part of my life's journey, an adventure in self-discovery and purpose. And it all began with a teenager's curiosity and a heart filled with a desire to make a difference.

The history of opium use is a story of transformation—evolving from a potent medicinal compound and recreational substance to a widely misused and addictive narcotic.

Historically, opium's use in medicine cannot be understated. It contains various alkaloids, including morphine, codeine, and thebaine, all of which possess potent analgesic, or pain-relieving, properties. Opium was often the go-to choice for alleviating pain resulting from injuries, surgeries, and various medical conditions. Its sedative attributes were also harnessed to induce sleep and mitigate anxiety, providing much-needed relief in numerous instances.

Opium's influence stretched beyond the medical realm, pervading social gatherings and religious ceremonies across many cultures. Its allure lay in its euphoric and relaxing effects, offering a sense of well-being, pleasure, and a temporary refuge from the stressors of daily life. Creatives often turned to opium to stimulate imaginative thinking and deepen introspection, claiming it inspired their work.

Despite its medicinal and recreational uses, opium's darker side—its addictive nature—became apparent. Prolonged use of opium and the opioids derived from it, such as morphine and heroin, revealed the detrimental effects associated with their misuse. Chronic misuse can lead to opioid addiction, a serious condition characterized by compulsive drug-seeking behavior and an inability to control or stop opioid use.

As the physical and psychological dependence on opioids develops, discontinuing their use without proper support becomes increasingly difficult. Complications can escalate to life-threatening proportions, with opioid overdoses necessitating immediate medical intervention. The implications of opioid addiction extend beyond the individual, having profound social and economic repercussions on families and communities.

As my work in the Golden Triangle unfolded, I became acutely aware of this delicate balance—opium as a source of income for impoverished communities on one hand, and a destructive, life-altering substance on the other. The challenge was not merely about introducing alternative crops; it was about disentangling the web of socio-economic and psychological factors that held these communities in the grip of opium cultivation. It was a complex mission, one that called for sensitivity, understanding, and sustainable solutions.

As my journey with the hill tribes progressed, so did my understanding of opium's devastating effects on these communities. It was during this period that I first came across a rather unconventional approach to treating opioid addiction: psychedelic therapy. While still in its nascent stages, research in the field suggested potential benefits of psychedelics in treating addiction.

Psychedelics, including substances like psilocybin and LSD, when administered in a therapeutic context, appeared to modulate the very brain circuits and neurotransmitter systems related to addiction. This compelling intersection of neuroscience and therapy piqued my interest, giving me hope that we could potentially offer these communities a novel means to break free from the cycle of addiction. Yet, the work was cut out for us: a lot more research and understanding was required before these therapies could be made widely available and accepted.

Parallel to my burgeoning interest in psychedelic therapy, my experience as a volunteer in the Golden Triangle was transforming me in ways I had not anticipated. Being the youngest participant, I was often on the receiving end of wisdom, knowledge, and guidance shared by the older members of our team. My aunt's adventurous spirit was a beacon guiding us through our efforts, her leadership a masterclass in resilience and altruism.

New friendships blossomed amid our shared purpose, reinforcing the ethos of our time: "Here, there are no strangers, only new friends we have just met." I am eternally grateful for these friendships, for the shared laughs, tears, and dreams, and for the collective drive that pushed us to make a positive change.

My college classmates joined our cause, inspired by the same principles that had led us to volunteer. My reputation as the 'class rebel' allowed me to recruit students who shared our passion for change. Each new recruit brought fresh perspectives and energy, further strengthening our resolve.

Reflecting on this period of my life, I realize it was a time of profound self-discovery. The seeds of the healer within me were being sown, nurtured by my exposure to the hardships and resilience of the hill tribes. But it would take several more decades before I fully comprehended my purpose, before I truly understood the healer I was meant to be. This realization would come only after more experiences, more learning, and more growth. But for now, I was on a journey, guided by a sense of adventure, a thirst for knowledge, and a desire to make a difference.

Situated amidst the breathtaking landscapes of the Golden Triangle, in the Mae Hong Son province of Thailand, lies Ban Nam Rin, a Lisu village. Known for their deep connection to nature and a rich cultural heritage rooted in the use of medicinal plants, the Lisu tribe is truly a gem in the annals of human history.

Tracing their origins back to Tibet, the Lisu people migrated through Burma before finally settling in the northern regions of Thailand. The journey through diverse landscapes and cultures left a mark on the tribe's genetic expression—a phenomenon we understand today as epigenetics. The differences between the Lisu communities in Burma and Thailand are intriguing, particularly the nuances in dialect, mindset, and life philosophy, revealing how environmental factors contribute to the evolution of human societies.

Nature plays a central role in Lisu life. They prefer to settle near bodies of water and within forest expanses, a testament to their deep bond with the natural world. Every village has its unique set of ceremonial plants and a shrine dedicated to the guardian spirit, who is believed to shield the village, maintain peace, and ward off troubles. Unlike some other tribes, the Lisu value stability, seldom migrating and choosing instead to establish and grow their communities over generations.

Spiritual beliefs run deep in Lisu culture. Ancestral spirits, forest spirits, house spirits, and reverence for natural elements like the sun, moon, and trees define their spiritual landscape. They also believe in ghosts and practice shamanism. Shamans, seen as intermediaries, bridge the gap between the human and spirit worlds.

Typically, a Lisu village comprises around a hundred households. They operate under a unique governance structure that lacks a formal political system. Instead, respect for elders, a tradition passed down through generations, is at the core of their social order. General rules are established through consensus. One interesting practice among the Lisu is intermarriage within bloodlines, often between cousins. The tribe practices monogamy, and a woman, once married, is considered her husband's property.

Lisu attire is a visual treat, rich in color and detail. Women typically wear a blue or green tunic with wide red sleeves, paired with knee-length black trousers, occasionally adorned with red leggings. The tunic is embellished with intricate, handcrafted details. Men, on the other hand, usually don simple black jackets with blue or green trousers, cinched at the waist with a red sash. On ceremonial occasions, their attire transforms into a vibrant display of velvet or satin, punctuated with silver buttons and other silver jewelry.

Agriculture is the bedrock of the Lisu economy, with opium traditionally being a major cash crop. As volunteers, we introduced the tribe to other grains like rice and wheat, educating them on sustainable farming practices, one village at a time. Over three decades have passed since then, and I cannot help but wonder how much the Lisu's agricultural practices have evolved.

The Lisu people's way of life has constantly adapted over time, reflecting their resilience, deep-rooted traditions, beliefs, and their ability to adapt to the world around them. Their rich cultural tapestry continues to captivate and inspire to this day.

Ahmee, a leading figure in the Lisu community at Mae Nam Rin, became an indispensable liaison for us. She was about five feet tall, always smiling, and dressed in traditional Lisu clothing—vibrant blue with dashes of other colors. An adept coordinator, she organized all our interactions and activities with the villagers - men, women, and children alike. Whenever we visited to provide educational resources or aid, Ahmee's humble home served as our welcoming hub.

Reaching her house was an adventure in itself. Our journey involved navigating challenging terrains and ascending steep hills on narrow trails. The cheerful laughter of barefoot children playing in the hills reverberated in the background, crafting a lively, homey ambiance.

Ahmee's residence was a quaint, wooden structure,

reminiscent of a treehouse. The roof was a beautiful, grass-woven tapestry of craftsmanship. Inside, the space was open and communal, with sleeping, sitting, and cooking areas flowing into one another. Bathroom facilities were an outhouse outside the main structure. Lacking modern amenities like electricity and running water, the house exemplified simplicity. Candlelight cast a cozy ambiance in the evenings, a clay stove offered fire for cooking, and rainwater collected for consumption, cooking, and cleaning embodied the community's resourcefulness. Ahmee's home illustrated the harmonious relationship the Lisu people shared with nature.

My understanding of psychedelic plants, particularly opium, and their cultural significance within the Lisu tribe was initially limited. Opium held a ritualistic role among the Lisu people, consumed by men, women, and even children before and after work. This practice was deeply embedded in their customs. However, by the 1980s, Thailand had reclassified opium as a controlled substance, banning its use.

This shift in legislation represented changing societal attitudes towards substances like opium and the need to address potential health risks associated with its use. It marked a transition in how such substances were perceived and controlled, underscoring the importance of protecting community health and well-being.

As we integrated into the village and worked alongside the Lisu people, we observed the cultural transformation unfolding in response to these societal changes. It was a period of transition and exploration, as the community sought new approaches and alternatives to enhance their lives while preserving their rich cultural heritage.

Throughout my college years, I dedicated my summer breaks and holidays to this project. Even after graduation, I continued to work with the Lisu community for several more years, a testament to the profound impact this experience had on my life.

As I continued to work with the Lisu community, it was impossible to overlook the relentless march of modernization encroaching upon their traditional way of life. This reality isn't limited to secluded communities such as hill tribes; it's a global phenomenon that impacts us all. The ability to step back and observe these changes from an outsider's perspective can be revelatory.

Take the introduction of running water and electricity, for instance. These advancements undoubtedly bring conveniences and potentially enhance our quality of life, but they also carry unforeseen consequences. Modern technologies such as television, smartphones, and social media have profoundly impacted our societies. They trigger shifts in values, alter our relationships with nature, and transform our belief systems.

These changes mean that certain cultural practices risk being gradually swept away. For instance, shamanic traditions may fade as younger generations, lured by the allure of urban life, leave their mountain homes. The distinctive charm of handmade clothing and traditional designs becomes scarcer as the tide of modernization rolls in.

Nonetheless, it's crucial to understand that modernization is a part of the grand human narrative. It is a fundamental aspect of our evolution that affects not only us but other life forms and the planet itself. We are continually caught in a state of flux, our cultures and societies morphing and adapting under the influence of modernity. This process, a dance between tradition and transformation, has been in play for millions of years and will continue to shape our world within our unique timelines and spaces.

Simultaneously, in parallel to observing these cultural shifts, our team of students and alumni was busy setting up medical screenings and health education initiatives. Recognizing the severe shortage of medical and healthcare professionals in these rural areas, we coordinated with alumni who had graduated and were working in these regions. We joined forces with local clinics, government health centers, and mobile health initiatives to offer our volunteer services.

We planned these activities on a monthly basis, or as frequently as possible. The aim was to bridge the gap in healthcare services and educate these communities about health and well-being. Our efforts reflected a belief in the importance of ensuring the health and welfare of these rural communities as they navigated the changing tides of modernization, just as we strived to preserve and understand their unique cultural heritage.

Opium has wielded a complex and influential role in Thailand, significantly impacting its social fabric, particularly in the northern regions, where opium cultivation was widespread. The substance wove itself into the tapestry of the communities, influencing social norms, traditions, and cultural practices. Its use became intertwined with rituals, medicinal applications, and social gatherings, shaping social interactions and customs in profound ways.

The Golden Triangle, the notorious region straddling the borders of Thailand, Laos, and Myanmar, has a historic reputation for its role in the global illicit drug trade. Opium was its infamous mainstay. Thailand, acting as a significant transit point, faced a series of challenges associated with this trade: smuggling, distribution, and widespread addiction problems. The cultivation and production of opium within the region contributed to a flood of illegal drugs within Thailand and rippling far beyond its borders.

The ramifications of opium use, and the availability of opioids derived from it, led to considerable public health and addiction challenges within Thailand. The country saw substance abuse, addiction, and associated health issues seep into the lives of individuals, families, and communities. The misuse of opium and opioids could result in severe health consequences, including physical dependence, overdose, and profound effects on morality, legal standing, and overall quality of life.

Faced with this multifaceted crisis, Thailand recognized the need for a nuanced solution. They identified that a significant portion of opium farmers were caught in a vicious cycle of poverty and dependence on the lucrative opium trade. Consequently, they launched alternative development programs aiming to break this cycle. These initiatives were designed to support affected communities by promoting sustainable agriculture, providing vocational training, and facilitating access to markets for legal crops. The overarching goal was to offer viable alternatives to opium cultivation and address the socio-economic factors that had perpetuated its production. By tackling the issue at its roots, the hope was to usher in lasting change, steering these communities towards a healthier, more sustainable future.

It was the wave initiatives that swept me into the Golden Triangle, and allowed me to etch beautiful memories into my mind. One particular summer break, our adventurous spirits led us, a small contingent of Mahidol University students, to take on a formidable challenge: trekking up Doi Chiang Dao. This limestone giant, the third highest mountain in Thailand, shrouded in a blanket of ethereal sea fog and teeming with an array of wildlife, beckoned us with its unique highland flora and mesmerizing fields of opium poppy.

Our week-long camping expedition traversing the high mountain range was an unparalleled experience, a testament to the captivating beauty of the natural world. Despite the thin air, a result of altitudes reaching over 7,000 feet above sea level, we persisted in our journey. Although we lacked the coca leaves used by trekkers ascending Machu Picchu to mitigate the effects of high altitude, the breathtaking surroundings provided ample motivation. Trekking through vast fields of opium poppies in bloom for days was a sight that both awed and intrigued us.

The allure of nature holds an indescribable power. It transcends the physical exertion, the pain, the sweat, the fatigue, rejuvenating our spirits and allowing us to immerse ourselves in the sensory tapestry of the environment. We tuned into the harmonious melodies of the forest, breathed in the fragrant air permeated with floral and earthy scents, and felt the gentle brush of the breeze and the kiss of moisture on our skin. In this seemingly ordinary state of existence, I found myself experiencing an extraordinary communion with nature. I was, for a moment, floating in a dreamlike state, surrounded by the ethereal beauty of the opium fields. And all this without touching, consuming, or inhaling any opium substance. This mystifying experience, to this day, perplexes me. How could merely being amidst the opium fields evoke such surreal sensations? The enigma persists, and I continue to ponder, reflecting on the extraordinary power of nature and its mysterious influences.

Looking back on that experience, a unique type of trouble comes to mind. The immense beauty of the natural environment held us spellbound, even as it posed significant challenges. After a grueling 72 hours without bathing, scant food and water, and sleeping on thin blankets within a tent, my shadow side emerged, craving physical comfort in circumstances where it was scarcely available.

We had set off on this journey with bare essentials, each carrying a minimal amount of supplies, with the intent of reaching the peak of the mountain within three days. However, halfway to our goal, as the summit began to loom large, my anxiety-ridden mind started to protest, declaring that it could go no further. Fatigue enveloped me, hunger gnawed incessantly at my stomach, and the blisters adorning my feet intensified the discomfort. I found myself reduced to tears, like a distraught child, contemplating surrender.

But surrender was not a viable option. Retracing my steps alone would merely prolong the hardship, as the journey back would take another three days, if not longer. Advancing with the team meant reaching the summit and descending the other side in a similar timeframe, perhaps slightly more. In the midst of this conundrum, my desire to capitulate felt both juvenile and irrational.

This ordeal served as a tough lesson in mental fortitude. It reminded me how our minds can beguile us into abandoning our ambitions when the journey becomes tough. Yet amidst the struggle, I uncovered a wellspring of resilience within me, a resource I had been unaware of. Despite the physical and emotional strain, I chose to persevere, drawing strength from my team's collective resolve and the mesmerizing beauty enveloping us.

In retrospect, it was the acceptance of discomfort and the defiance against my own self-doubt that led me to a profound sense of achievement. The journey instilled in me the understanding that genuine growth often sprouts from the most challenging circumstances, and it is during these testing times that we unearth our latent reserves of strength and resilience.

As I advanced through life, I came to realize that when negative or contradictory emotions overtake us and render us vulnerable and scared, everything tends to appear larger, often skewed towards the worst-case scenario. At times, the overpowering negativity seems unfounded. It is in these moments that the strength of clear thinking and the capability to make conscious decisions become paramount.

Troubles can emerge from our shadow selves, the aspects of our personality we may not fully comprehend, or from internal conflicts born out of fear—fear of pain, discomfort, darkness, or even the anticipation of fear itself. The list is extensive.

However, it's truly awe-inspiring to witness the shift in emotions once a decision is made. Sometimes, this change occurs as a spontaneous awakening, while at other times, it is directed by a higher consciousness or merely the presence and support of courageous individuals surrounding us.

When contemplating past experiences, the mind possesses a striking capability to recall distressing moments vividly. The amygdala, the brain area associated with memory and emotional experiences, diligently performs its task. However, when we consciously work to rewire this part of our brain, it doesn't mean we erase the experiences entirely. Instead, we acquire the ability to revisit events and circumstances with altered emotional responses. This is a critical insight I have gained lately— the understanding that traumatic emotions can be mitigated through the rewiring of our brains and minds, given suitable support and guidance.

Recognizing the potency of our thoughts and decisions,

coupled with the possibility of rewiring our emotional responses, instills a renewed sense of hope and empowerment. It serves as a reminder that even amidst challenging times, we possess the capacity to shift our perspectives, heal our emotional wounds, and foster emotional resilience.

As time passed, my experiences in these projects and interactions with the community evolved into something profoundly deep and meaningful. I found myself enchanted by the pure mindset of the indigenous people, the unrivaled beauty of nature, and the unpretentious simplicity of their lifestyle. This journey induced reflection on the essence of life, what genuinely matters, and what we truly require to live a fulfilled life. It elicited a deep appreciation for life itself, nurturing an attitude of cherishing every moment and expressing gratitude for all that life bestows upon us.

Throughout the years of supporting these projects and engaging with the hill tribe community, the entire village turned into a family to me. We forged a strong bond, a deep connection that echoed a sense of "connectedness," a sentiment frequently associated with certain psychedelic compounds. But such a state of connection was achieved here without consuming any such substances. The authentic relationships we developed through shared experiences, coupled with our deep appreciation for the natural world, culminated in a profound sense of unity and interconnectedness.

The collective experiences we shared during these trips played a pivotal role in shaping who we are today. For me, the impact was profound—it influenced my personal growth in ways I hadn't imagined. Changes unfolded gradually, guided by our inclinations and where we directed our energy. The focus we laid on making meaningful contributions to society and humanity started to form the overarching theme of our lives.

Looking back at the years that have passed, I recognize that this theme has crystallized into my life's purpose, my calling, the essence of my existence – to be here, in service, dedicated to societal healing throughout my lifetime. Everyone will eventually discover their own theme, what they are here to contribute. It is a journey of self-discovery, of finding the unique purpose that resonates within, guiding our actions, and shaping the way we lead our lives.

Life is guided by time and the ever-changing canvas of opportunities. As it propels forward, we adapt, transitioning into what comes next, drawing on the reservoir of lessons and experiences we have amassed along the way. Each step, each encounter, and each experience becomes a valuable foundation upon which we construct the succeeding chapter of our journey.

The growth and wisdom derived from previous experiences continue to influence and support us as we embrace new opportunities, navigating the continuously evolving path of life. Thus, it's time to harness these learnings and move on, with our hearts full of anticipation for the other opportunities that await us.

Cannabis

My introduction to cannabis wasn't in the form that most might imagine. It wasn't a smoky encounter at a party, nor an illicit transaction in some shadowy corner. In fact, I have never smoked in my life. My rendezvous with cannabis took place during a college summer break, in the humble setting of Thailand's countryside, where I encountered cannabis in a form quite different from the typical Western narrative.

At the time, I was actively participating in the student union, leading various initiatives to support underprivileged communities. Our efforts took us to remote clinics, impoverished villages, and underserved schools. These rural excursions were both a voyage of cultural discovery and a gastronomic adventure. We eagerly sampled local cuisines, with street food offering a cornucopia of flavors that were an absolute treat to our palates.

Among the many local specialties, one dish that left a lasting impression was a particular noodle soup. It was unique not just for its tantalizing flavor, but for its ability to lift our spirits in a way that no other food could. Consumption was invariably followed by a wave of light-heartedness, triggering infectious smiles, laughter, and a relaxed demeanor among our group. The dish was almost magical in its effects.

It wasn't until later that I unraveled the secret behind these mood-enhancing effects. The magical ingredient that transformed an ordinary soup into an elixir of joy was, to my surprise, cannabis, locally referred to as Ganja or Gancha. This herb was a common addition in certain regional Thai cuisines and did not draw any unusual attention from the locals, further adding to its mystique.

Cannabis is a plant with deep roots in the culture and history of my birth country. This remarkable plant has found its way into the traditional medicine practices of Thailand for centuries, featured in over 200 formulas of Thai Traditional Medicine. Embedded in the fabric of our ancient healing systems, cannabis has played an integral role in maintaining wellness and balance within Thai communities for generations.

My curiosity about cannabis was first piqued in the early 2000s, sparked by conversations with friends who touted its potential as an alternative remedy for anxiety and pain management. Despite this newfound interest, learning that it was classified as a controlled substance prompted me to maintain a cautious distance from it. I distinctly recall a sense of apprehension when a friend offered me a small container of cannabis-infused balm to try.

The years that followed marked a turning point in my

understanding of cannabis, bringing me into close quarters with individuals whose lives were inextricably tied to this plant. This phase saw my role evolve from a bystander to an active participant seeking to unravel the complexities surrounding cannabis legalization.

The turn of the 21st century ushered in the legalization of medical cannabis. However, cultivation of the plant by private individuals was still prohibited. During this period, I noted a surge in the number of medical cannabis dispensaries, particularly in California. The increased focus on research and studies further piqued my interest, propelling me deeper into the world of cannabis.

In 2010, my perspective shifted dramatically when a friend, who was living as a "fugitive," approached me for help. I discovered that he had been covertly cultivating cannabis plants and extracting their compounds for personal use to manage his epilepsy. His story was striking —he had been using cannabis as a safe and non-addictive form of self-care for over a decade, not selling it or causing harm to anyone. It raised crucial questions in my mind: Why was the use of a plant that seemingly had such beneficial properties illegal? How did this situation come about?

Spurred by these questions, I embarked on a quest to study the properties of these plants, a journey that I continue to pursue to this day.

My exploration took a significant turn in 2012 when I had the opportunity to learn from a family deeply involved in cannabis cultivation and traditional medicine processing. Simultaneously, I stepped into the realm of

Thai traditional medicine, discovering preparations that incorporated cannabis. This marked the beginning of my hands-on experience with this multifaceted plant, and it paved the way for deeper understanding and involvement.

The rescheduling of cannabis in the U.S. law represented a significant turning point, granting me the opportunity to deepen my understanding of this fascinating plant within the confines of legality. This period ushered in a phase of hands-on learning about the myriad aspects of cannabis—from its genetics, cultivation, and processing, to the formulation and medical science that surround this unique plant.

Cannabis quickly became one of the most captivating plants I've ever encountered. I spent countless hours observing its behavior and processes, particularly its fascinating capability for epigenetic modification—akin to humans and other life forms. The environment in which the plants grow can significantly influence the variety of compounds they produce. Cannabis is a chemical powerhouse, generating a staggering array of over 400 compounds, including cannabinoids, flavonoids, terpenoids, amino acids, fatty acids, vitamins, minerals, and other alkaloids. This extensive chemical profile contributes to its diverse medicinal properties and applications.

While the psychoactive effects of cannabis, mainly attributable to tetrahydrocannabinol (THC), are widely known, it's essential to note that its impact on consciousness differs significantly from classic psychedelics such as psilocybin and lysergic acid diethylamide (LSD).

Ego dissolution, sometimes referred to as "ego death," is a phenomenon that individuals may encounter during intense psychedelic experiences. This term describes a complete loss of subjective self-identity and is often accompanied by feelings of unity, interconnectedness, and oneness with the universe.

Contrastingly, cannabis, even though it possesses psychoactive properties, doesn't typically induce the same degree of ego dissolution or the sense of universal connectedness often reported with the use of classic psychedelics.

Classic psychedelics like psilocybin (found in magic mushrooms) and LSD primarily target the serotonin 2A receptor (5-HT2A), thought to be responsible for inducing these profound experiences. The interaction of these compounds with our neurochemistry can result in significant alterations in consciousness and perception, leading to experiences often described as mystical or transcendental.

As I continued to explore the world of cannabis and its effects, I grew increasingly aware of these distinctions, deepening my understanding of its unique potential and place within the broader spectrum of consciousness-altering substances.

The endocannabinoid system (ECS), a complex cell-signaling structure integral to maintaining physiological homeostasis, plays a pivotal role in understanding cannabis's impacts. Interestingly, it was named after the plant that led to its discovery—cannabis, highlighting the plant's significance in modern scientific understanding. The ECS is intertwined with numerous bodily processes, including pain regulation, memory, mood, appetite, stress management, sleep, metabolism, immune function, and reproductive function.

Notably, cannabis impacts our physical and mental states differently than other psychedelic compounds, primarily in terms of the receptors it binds to trigger healing or repairing cascades in the body. Over years of research, presentations, and efforts to distill complex science into simpler terms, I have come to appreciate cannabis as one of the most extraordinary plants. The uniqueness of cannabis lies in its ability to activate the endocannabinoid system and trigger a multitude of other chemical and biological pathways, showcasing its potent potential for therapeutic applications.

In a significant development, Thailand became the first Asian country to legalize medical cannabis in 2019. During this time, I had the opportunity to invite a group of scientists to a conference in Thailand. It was also during this period that I had my first experience with a high dosage of THC, the psychoactive compound extracted from cannabis plants, provided in capsule form. The effects were far more potent than I anticipated.

The psychoactive state induced by a single 10 mg THC capsule lingered for approximately 72 hours. The effects were reminiscent of being on a rolling boat in the midst of vast ocean waves. Through this experience, I understood that my genetic makeup caused my system to hold onto the psychoactive effects for such an extended period. Interestingly, I did not experience any other notable effects, whether desirable or undesirable.

At one point in my research journey, I believed I was on the brink of decoding the cannabis mystery by comparing the endocannabinoid system to the Chinese meridian system. The healing concepts shared some striking similarities— the energy balance, the management of excess or deficiency, and the ability to treat a range of conditions, from straightforward ailments like anxiety to life-threatening illnesses such as cancer.

While there is still much to explore and discover, current evidence reveals the intricate chemical pathways or receptors that the compounds in the cannabis plant, including cannabinoids, can modulate. For instance, the well-known CB1 and CB2 receptors have proven to play significant roles in our understanding of the plant's influence on our bodies and our overall health. These findings offer valuable insights into how cannabis interacts with our bodily systems and its potential therapeutic applications.

The two most studied receptors in the endocannabinoid system, CB1 and CB2, are indeed key players in the effects of cannabis. CB1 receptors are found mostly in the central nervous system but also in other tissues including the liver, kidneys, and lungs. THC has a high affinity for CB1 receptors, and this interaction results in the psychoactive effects of cannabis. CB2 receptors, on the other hand, primarily reside in the immune system and hematopoietic cells, playing a significant role in inflammation and immune response. THC and CBD can interact with CB2 receptors, although CBD has a lower affinity for these receptors than THC.

Many illnesses are triggered by inflammation or immune disorders. Understanding that cannabis binds to these two crucial receptors, CB1 and CB2, which play significant roles in these processes, we begin to understand how cannabis supports our healing and restoration.

But the healing prowess of cannabis extends beyond these two receptors. It also interacts with several other key receptors, giving us insight into how it aids in healing a wide variety of conditions. For example, certain cannabinoids can activate peroxisome proliferator-activated receptors (PPARs), nuclear receptors that regulate cellular function and metabolism, potentially impacting conditions like Alzheimer's disease, diabetes, and certain types of cancer.

Cannabinoids, including THC and CBD, influence certain types of transient receptor potential cation channels (TRP channels) such as TRPV1, TRPV2, TRPA1, and TRPM8. These ion channels are located on the cell membrane of various tissues and are involved in several physiological processes, including pain perception, body temperature regulation, and inflammation.

Cannabinoids, particularly CBD, have been found to potentiate glycine receptors, which are implicated in pain processing. Some research suggests that cannabinoids can enhance the effects of certain opioids, potentially through indirect interaction with opioid receptors. This interaction could contribute to the pain-modulating effects of cannabis.

Furthermore, CBD is believed to inhibit the reuptake of adenosine, which leads to an increase in the availability of adenosine in the brain, potentially decreasing the inflammatory response. Lastly, CBD is also thought to act upon the 5-HT1A serotonin receptor, which may be responsible for some of its reported anti-anxiety and antidepressant effects. While most other psychedelic compounds act on the 5-HT2 receptors affecting sensory perception, cannabis uniquely interacts with the 5-HT1A receptor, contributing to its calming effect.

These above paragraphs may seem like they veer towards science fiction, but they represent a reality backed by numerous scientific research studies. The truly incredible part, which might appear to be 'beyond reality,' is the capacity of cannabis to support the healing of hundreds of conditions.

Cannabis stands apart from many traditional psychedelic compounds such as psilocybin or LSD, offering a unique set of potential benefits. With professional care and supervision, medical cannabis could become a powerful tool in managing, and potentially even reversing, various disease conditions. It's important to make a clear distinction here—this isn't about recreational cannabis products that one might find at dispensaries. Those are more akin to over-the-counter products. Instead, in a therapeutic context, cannabis can play a crucial role in addressing an array of health concerns.

This, however, is just the tip of the iceberg when it

comes to the healing potential of plant-based therapies. On the other side of the spectrum, substances such as psilocybin and San Pedro (which contains mescaline), traditionally classified as psychedelics, offer a deeper potential for psychological healing. These substances can make significant contributions to the field of mental health, and even beyond - to spiritual systems, personal growth, and the fostering of a compassionate and mindful society.

These psychedelics can help restore aspects of our humanity that we may have lost or forgotten, guiding us toward a higher consciousness of what it truly means to be human. At the very least, they can support mental health, a fundamental need for every individual in society.

The individual impact of each of these substances is distinct, yet they can also complement each other in various ways. We humans are unique, and the way these compounds interact with us is highly individualized. As such, the use of these substances is a personalized journey and requires further exploration and ongoing self-development, which, in itself, is an endless process.

With a deeper understanding of these powerful substances, we are better equipped to navigate this journey. Our next topic of discussion will carry us further along this path, as we dive into the other psychedelics that have played a significant role in my personal and professional life.

Psilocybin

In the realm of plant medicine, each substance seems to have a unique spirit or essence. For instance, Ayahuasca is frequently dubbed the "vine of the soul". The moniker, resonating with deep ancestral wisdom, denotes a connection to the innermost corners of our consciousness and the spirit world.

If Ayahuasca is the vine of the soul, psilocybin could arguably be portrayed as a "messenger of the stars." This depiction, brimming with celestial connotations, suggests a profound bond to the cosmic realms and higher dimensions.

This concept elicits images of boundless cosmic expanses, hinting at psilocybin's potential to foster transcendent experiences. The metaphor paints psilocybin as a gateway or conduit, facilitating communion with cosmic consciousness and offering an individual access to insights and perspectives beyond ordinary perception.

Yet, this portrayal of psilocybin arises from a mystical viewpoint rather than a strictly scientific one. This perspective sees the world not just as a collection of quantifiable phenomena, but as a tapestry interwoven with mysterious, awe-inspiring aspects of existence. Psilocybin, viewed through this mystical lens, isn't merely a psychoactive substance affecting neurotransmitters in the brain. Instead, it is seen as a cosmic messenger capable of unveiling the interconnectedness of the universe and transporting us into dimensions of consciousness far removed from our everyday reality.

Personally, I enjoy studying not only the science, but also into the mystical aspect of psilocybin, examining the ways it can catalyze profound transformations and open doors to expansive realms of consciousness.

Psilocybin induces alterations in mental states, perception of time and space, and self-identity. Once ingested, psilocybin is metabolized into psilocin, a molecule structurally akin to serotonin and known for its anxiety-reducing and mystical-like effects.

Recent studies have observed psilocin's ability to transiently disrupt neural connectivity, which effectively initiates a 'rewiring' process within the brain. This disruption impacts various brain functions, including self-referential thinking, introception, memory retrieval, and future imagery. By disrupting the connection between the amygdala (responsible for fear memory) and cognitive processes, psilocin can potentially support the therapeutic processing of traumatic experiences.

Despite its "otherworldly" effects, psilocybin can be found growing in some rather humble, low-down places. My early encounters with psilocybin were less about conscious exploration and more about youthful curiosity. As a city-bred child, my visits to the Thai countryside were exhilarating adventures, an invitation to explore a world far removed from my urban routine. Hiking in the lush forests was a personal favorite pastime, an activity that piqued my interest in the array of lifeforms thriving in the woods.

During this period, Thailand was primarily known as one of Asia's leading rice producers. Water buffaloes were vital assets in plowing the fields, becoming a familiar sight across the countryside. In their wake, small, slim, brown mushrooms sprouted from the fertile dung, capturing my youthful interest. Adults would often warn us against ingesting these mushrooms, cautioning that they could induce states of intoxication. I found it odd that they thought it necessary to warn me away from eating anything that grew out of buffalo dung, but took the warning to heart nonetheless. Little did I know, these were my early introductions to what would later be known as "magic mushrooms," the famous Psilocybe cubensis.

Psilocybe cubensis is one of the most widely recognized species of psilocybin-containing mushrooms, with a native range believed to span Southeast Asia, including Thailand, Vietnam, and Cambodia. Like tiny cosmic messengers, these magic mushrooms have the potential to invite us into extraordinary states of consciousness.

Fast forward a few decades, and Thailand emerged as one of the top tourist destinations worldwide, becoming a gathering ground for Western travelers. Among the numerous attractions dotting the country, the island of

Koh Phangan held a unique charm. With a human history dating back over 2,000 years, the island had once served as a fishing outpost and a coconut plantation in the 19th century.

In the 1970s, Koh Phangan, along with other Thai islands, turned into a sanctuary for backpackers and hippies seeking an alternative, free-spirited lifestyle. Drawn by the island's pristine beaches, untouched nature, and tranquil ambiance, these wanderers arrived by boat, immersing themselves in the island's serene beauty. The emergence of this era also marked the establishment of various spiritual communities and meditation retreat centers across the island. The island transitioned from a simple coconut plantation to a spiritual haven, a place of introspection and transformative experiences, part of which was facilitated by the humble Psilocybe cubensis.

In the late 1980s, Koh Phangan bore witness to a unique phenomenon, a testament to the allure of its charm. A small group of tourists, captivated by the island's beauty under the full moon, decided to host a beach party at Haad Rin, a picturesque stretch on the island's southern tip. This event marked the birth of what would come to be known globally as the "Full Moon Party."

The Full Moon Party started as an intimate gathering, with music, dancing, and fire shows gracing the beach under the full moon. Word spread about these magical celebrations, and their reputation grew, attracting more visitors locally and internationally. The event soon became a monthly spectacle, drawing thousands of enthusiastic partygoers with its vibrant atmosphere and rhythmic music.

Koh Phangan and its neighboring island, Koh Samui, gained a reputation for a unique offering: magic mushroom smoothies and drinks. These beverages contained the psilocybin mushrooms I had once been warned about as a child. Popular among a segment of tourists, these magic mushroom-infused concoctions became a sought-after psychedelic experience, despite the murky legal status of psilocybin in Thailand.

As a medical doctor with a profound interest in psychoactive plants and compounds, I couldn't help finding this trend disconcerting. The ecosystem surrounding these mushroom smoothies seemed to foster harm over healing, diverting psilocybin from its potential therapeutic role.

Although I've never used magic mushrooms recreationally, I have a profound respect for these plants, considering them sacred entities with potential healing abilities. My scientific background and mystical leanings coalesce in my appreciation of psilocybin, viewing it as a nurturing force rather than a mere recreational substance.

Throughout my life journey, I've been led to explore medicinal plants, not by mere chance, but by a path of synchronicity. This path is rooted in a deep belief that knowledge is granted when earnestly sought. Over the years, I've had the privilege of learning from scientists and healers alike, which has broadened my understanding and amplified my curiosity about these incredible organisms and their potential to promote human healing and wellness.

Each step of my research and exploration has contributed to my comprehension of the extraordinary healing potential inherent in psychedelic medicine. This knowledge continues to evolve and deepen, echoing an ancient wisdom that remains just as pertinent in our modern world.

I am humbled by the lessons that these incredible tools for personal growth continue to teach me. They inspire me to contribute to the well-being of others through responsible and informed exploration of these substances.

I once participated in a week-long retreat in the beautiful highlands of Jamaica, where I underwent three Psilocybin ceremonies—part of my ever-evolving quest to unlock what I call the psychedelic code. This complex code represents an understanding and insight into the therapeutic potential of psychedelics, which had been elusive despite my years of research and exploration.

I found the experience in Jamaica to be akin to the 21-day darkness retreat, condensed into a mere 7 days. The ceremonies dramatically altered my sensory perception and consciousness, yielding a thought-provoking impact.

In each session, I began with a dose of 2.5 grams of dried psilocybin, incrementally increasing the dosage by one gram for the subsequent sessions, with a 48-hour interval in between. For the uninitiated, 4.5 grams may seem like a high dose, but there is more to this journey than simply ingesting the mushrooms.

One must approach such experiences with mindful self-preparation, clear intentions, managed expectations, and judicious selection of one's company, including the facilitators guiding the session. The quality and preparation of the compounds themselves are also critical, along with countless other nuances that contribute to the holistic experience. These factors, often referred to as 'set', 'setting', and 'beyond', greatly influence the depth and outcome of the journey.

The recent Psilocybin experience for me was akin to a 'wow of awakening', echoing the profound enlightenment I underwent 21 years ago during the darkness retreat. The resonance and significance of this recent journey reverberates deeply within me.

The retreat unfolded in the awe-inspiring landscape of an old plantation, nestled within Jamaica's lush rainforests and towering mountains. A team of contemporary Western shamans and local Jamaican healers seamlessly fused traditional and modern practices to guide the retreat. The idyllic surroundings fostered a sense of peace, trust, and surrender, priming us for the transformative journey ahead.

The natural landscape resembled a mystical canvas, with the sky casting a riot of colors over the forested mountains. The air was alive with birdsong, while owls rested on trees, defying the daylight. Vibrant orchids added splashes of color, and giant hummingbirds flitted about in their quest for nectar. Refreshments, in the form of coconut water and herbal tea, were readily available, along with nutrient-rich superfoods to nourish the mind and body.

Suffice it to say, the setting portion of my "set and

setting" were ideal.

Each ceremony commenced with a customary cleansing ritual, using the smoke from burning sage. Participants, in a single file, underwent cleansing and selected their spaces for the session. Each was provided with a comfortable futon on the natural ground, complete with an eye mask and blanket. Hydration was emphasized, with each participant carrying their water bottle.

This meticulous attention to detail, creating a nurturing space, set the stage for a transformative journey with the medicine. It enabled us to immerse ourselves fully in the experience, free of distractions, and harness the healing potential of the Psilocybin ceremonies.

It was this trip to Jamaica that ignited a dramatic shift in my perception. This event proved to be an extraordinary synthesis of all my accumulated experiences over three decades. It was there, under the tropical sun of Jamaica in November 2022, that I experienced an epiphany — I cracked the Psychedelic Code. This breakthrough elicited an overwhelming sense of exhilaration, imbuing me with a renewed purpose to help others decipher their own psychedelic codes.

In Jamaica, I was reminded of a profound sense of unconditional love. This potent sensation is what I can only describe as a "cosmic orgasm." It's as if every single cell in my body vibrates in an ecstatic dance of existential bliss. The sensation comes in waves, recurring roughly every 45 minutes, taking control of my physical being as I can only stand back and observe, filled with immense joy. These moments of peak experience seem to micro-pulsate throughout my entire body, lasting for several intense minutes. They serve as bookmarks, reminders of the deep and powerful energies that flow through us when we're in tune with the universe.

I know that this sounds more euphoric than the typical human encounter with psilocybin, which is why I believe that the compound was not the only thing at work. My experience in Jamaica was the physical, mental, and spiritual culmination of my journey thus far, like a wave that had been building for decades finally broke while I was right at its crest. I believe that psilocybin has the potential to break similar waves for many people all around the globe.

Promising research conducted by renowned institutions worldwide indicates that Psilocybin has the potential to revolutionize our approach to mental health, specifically in treating cases of treatment-resistant depression. The studies involved participants undergoing meticulously guided psilocybin-assisted therapy sessions. These sessions were carried out in controlled settings under the supervision of trained professionals and were accompanied by comprehensive preparatory and integration therapy. This supportive framework aimed to equip participants with the necessary tools and guidance to navigate the entire process seamlessly.

The findings from these research initiatives have been highly encouraging. They suggest that a single or a handful of psilocybin-assisted therapy sessions can lead to significant and tangible reductions in depressive symptoms. More intriguingly, some participants reported experiencing long-term benefits that extended well beyond the therapy sessions.

Psilocybin's potential therapeutic impact stems not just from its ability to mitigate symptoms but also from its capacity to inspire transformational insights. By ushering in new perspectives and fostering a greater sense of personal meaning, psilocybin-assisted therapy can empower individuals to redefine their relationship with their inner selves. It can foster a stronger connection to the world around them, enabling them to navigate their emotional landscapes with greater resilience, insight, and acceptance.

Given these promising results, it is evident that the impact of psilocybin on global mental health paradigms could be profound and far-reaching. This potent compound holds the promise of not just addressing the symptoms of mental health disorders but also enabling a deeper exploration and healing of the underlying psychological and emotional terrains. Such an approach could lead to more enduring and holistic outcomes for individuals grappling with mental health challenges.

In the realm of end-of-life care—especially within palliative or near end-of-life settings—the focus traditionally lies in providing physical comfort, alleviating pain, and reducing mental and psychological distress. The emerging body of research indicates that psilocybin and other psychedelic substances may have significant roles to play in these critical areas. Furthermore, they may help individuals achieve a deeper understanding of the spiritual dimension of their experiences.

Psychedelic compounds have demonstrated potential in assisting individuals to navigate existential distress, offering comfort, and facilitating a peaceful transition during end-of-life stages. By addressing the spiritual and psychological dimensions of the human experience, these substances can contribute to enhancing the overall well-being and quality of life during end-of-life care.

As we continue to delve into the mysteries of psilocybin and its therapeutic potential, it is vital to approach it with respect, rigor, and a commitment to safety. After all, it is an extremely powerful medicine. With careful consideration of its applications and ethical use, we can unlock the full potential of this extraordinary compound to serve as a powerful ally in our quest for mental well-being and personal transformation. Psilocybin could be a holistic and compassionate guardian of our shared human experience – from the vibrancy of life to the tranquility at its end.

Deadline by Prognosis

Imagine being told that you have a mere thirty days left to exist. Suddenly, every second counts, every interaction matters, and each breath holds a significance it never did before. You might consider where you'd like to spend these dwindling moments, who you'd want beside you, and what dreams you'd chase down. Above all, consider this: how might such a revelation transform your state of mind?

"End-stage cancer", "terminally ill", "chronic illness" - such phrases carry immense weight in the realm of conventional medicine. Physicians use prognosis, often derived from extensive data and statistical patterns, to provide a glimpse into the patient's future health trajectory.

Yet, a prognosis, regardless of its grim nature, is not always a concrete expiration date stamped on a person's life. More often than not, it can morph into a self-imposed deadline, an invisible hourglass endlessly trickling down. We've all heard stories of medical verdicts that seem to eclipse all hope.

"You will need to take this medication for the rest of your life."

"You will live with this condition forever."

Or, the crushing, "There's nothing more we can do for you; your health will continue to deteriorate."

Such declarations, while often well-intentioned and grounded in fact, can sometimes overlook a critical element of the healing process - the power of hope. The role of hope in healing is neither anecdotal nor abstract; it's a crucial ingredient backed by significant empirical evidence and experiential data.

Hope is not just an emotion; it's a state of mind. It galvanizes the will to improve, to recover, to transcend beyond the limiting prognosis. It prepares us for the upward journey, stimulating the interplay of the mind and the physical body, a concept we've often underplayed in traditional medicine.

Diagnosis in conventional medicine is not always a precise science; its accuracy can vary significantly based on numerous factors. These can include the complexity of the condition at hand, the expertise and insights of the healthcare provider, the quality and sophistication of the available diagnostic tools and technology, and the clarity and comprehensiveness of the patient's symptoms and medical history.

Take, for instance, the diagnosis of cancer. A 2020 review published in "The American Journal of Surgical Pathology" found that the overall diagnostic accuracy rate for pathologists interpreting breast biopsy specimens was about 84.6%. While this may seem quite high, it leaves room for potential inaccuracies.

Even more sobering, a review of autopsy studies published in "BMJ Quality & Safety" in 2012 showed that major diagnostic errors that could lead to severe patient harm were evident in 10% of cases. These numbers are not intended to induce fear or skepticism, but rather to illuminate the complexity and fallibility inherent in the diagnostic process.

Developing a prognosis based on historical medical data is perhaps the best we can manage in terms of a "blanket policy." Basing decisions on broad data will result in equally broad decision-making, instead of intricate case-by-case assessments. It's important to note that the accuracy rate I mentioned was relatively high, and the harm rate relatively low. This is evidence of, when viewed as a whole, an effective system.

But why isn't it perfect? In matters of science and unconscious systems such as the human immune system, shouldn't our gaze into the future be crystal clear? Shouldn't it at least be closer to the accuracy of plotting a probe's course through the solar system? Unfortunately, there are too many variables in the human equation, and too many anomalies that we do not quite understand.

One of these anomalies is what's known as "Spontaneous healing." This refers to instances of significant improvement or complete recovery from a disease or condition that occur without medical intervention or where the improvement or recovery cannot be attributed to the treatments provided.

This fascinating phenomenon has been studied in numerous contexts, including spontaneous remission of cancer and spontaneous changes in other chronic diseases. A testament to this is the Spontaneous Remission Project initiated by the Institute of Noetic Sciences. This extensive database has gathered over 3,500 references from medical literature concerning cases of spontaneous remission, involving a variety of serious illnesses including cancer, heart defects, autoimmune diseases, and more.

My goal in this writing is not to criticize the diagnostic and prognosis process, but to focus on the inherent healing capacities we possess as individuals. By adopting a holistic and integrative approach to disease management, we can tap into these innate abilities. At the core of this process lies the formidable power of the mind.

To grasp this concept more fully, we need to plunge into the very genesis of diseases. Diseases don't spring up overnight. Each one unfolds through its unique process and timeline. In essence, the causes of diseases are diverse and multilayered. They may stem from infections, physical or psychological traumas, autoimmune reactions, chronic inflammation, or even unknown factors that continue to baffle the scientific community.

While some conditions can be managed and effectively cured, others may require more time and a broader spectrum of interventions. Some diseases might not be entirely curable but could be placed in a state of remission. This means that the disease continues to coexist with us but doesn't disrupt our physical or psychological equilibrium.

The pathways to healing, therefore, need not always culminate in a 'cure'. Sometimes, achieving a state of balance, where we peacefully coexist with our condition, is equally, if not more, therapeutic. And in this intricate journey of healing, the power of the mind plays an instrumental role.

So, how does one grapple with curing or maintaining diseases in remission? In conventional medicine, the response frequently revolves around the twin pillars of immunity and inflammation. The delicate balance lies in avoiding overstimulation of our immune system while ensuring it isn't compromised.

Inflammation can be seen as a body's warning system, signaling our physical or psychological systems to investigate and resolve non-functional areas before a disease manifests. Suppressing inflammation could consequently result in the loss of this vital warning signal. Yet, if we allow inflammation, whether physical or psychological (due to insult or trauma), to persist unchecked, it can pave the way for the emergence of diseases and illnesses.

Over the years, I have crossed paths with many patients diagnosed with a spectrum of diseases, from cancer to chronic illnesses, and those branded with a particular "deadline." As early as 2012, my primary protocol leaned heavily towards integrative medicine, blending techniques from medical qigong, HeartMath® , meditation, and lifestyle modification.

Astoundingly, many of these patients managed to shift their deadlines, with some even witnessing spontaneous healing and disease remission. As I dug deeper to comprehend this phenomenon, it became increasingly clear that simple practices enabling the mind to tap into its intrinsic capacity to restore balance do indeed work.

It is genuinely mesmerizing to witness the power of psycho-spiritual medicine and the innate capacity for healing and repairing when the right context and setting are provided.

I firmly believe that by cultivating a mindful approach and adopting the role of an observer in the face of life-altering events, we can potentially expedite and even bypass the painful grieving process. The power to rewire our thinking patterns and mental processing lies within long-term training and practice of the mind.

Dr. Roland Griffiths, one of the most renowned figures in the field of psychedelic science, eloquently captured a sentiment that deeply resonates with my daily practice: "Living in the present moment and cultivating a mindset of gratitude can sustain peace and enhance the quality of every second we have here on Earth."

Indeed, gratitude has been a guiding theme throughout my life. It has not only helped me navigate through struggles but has also allowed me to reinvent myself, forge ahead with determination, and manifest abundance and kindness on all levels of my existence.

Psychospiritual healing is a holistic healing process that embraces the interconnectedness of mind, body, and spirit in promoting overall well-being. This approach involves techniques that cater to not just physical issues but also emotional, psychological, and spiritual aspects of an individual.

The process employs an array of modalities, such as meditation, mindfulness, yoga, breathwork, prayer, and other spiritual practices. These techniques are believed to help alleviate stress, improve mental health, enhance immune system functionality, and promote an overall sense of well-being.

The interplay of determination, attitude, mindset, and the willingness to heal on patient recovery is a complex and multifaceted topic. These elements undeniably play critical roles in how people cope with illness, adhere to treatment, and maintain their quality of life.

Interestingly, both medical qigong meditation and The Monroe programs, which use guided visualization during non-ordinary states of consciousness, have been used to enhance the action of a certain aspect of the immune system against cancer cells or other abnormal cells.

T-cells, or T-lymphocytes, are a type of white blood cell that plays a crucial role in the immune system's response to infections, cancer, and chronic illnesses. They are an essential component of the adaptive immune system, which equips the body to recognize and respond to specific threats. The primary function of T-cells is to identify and destroy infected cells, cancer cells, or cells that have been invaded by pathogens.

This conscious interaction with the immune system only

further highlights the intricate connection between the mind and body and the role of psychospiritual practices in promoting overall health and well-being.

I recall my first encounter with spontaneous healing dating back to my days in medical school, an eye-opening experience that I would come across several times later in my career. However, the true embodiment of this phenomenon manifested when I began facilitating Medical Qigong retreats in the early 2000s. It was during these retreats that I gained hands-on experience in guiding patients to shift their mindset as a powerful tool for transforming their lives. This was the groundbreaking moment when I could tangibly see the 'deadline' being successfully extended for the first time.

Two decades ago, in Greenville, I embarked on a unique endeavor that would shape my journey in medicine and healing. It was a day retreat center, far removed from the sterile ambiance of a clinical setting. We consciously chose to refer to the individuals attending as "participants" rather than "patients," to emphasize their active role in the healing process. This was a period of exploration and growth within the realms of functional medicine, holistic medicine, integrative medicine, lifestyle medicine, and energy medicine. Our retreat incorporated practices like meditation, tai chi, yoga, and medical qigong. Located in a traditionally conservative Christian Bible Belt area, our center was nevertheless met with open minds and a community eager to embrace the reemerging interest in mind-body practices.

My primary focus during this period was providing an

opportunity for self-exploration across the physical, mental, social, and spiritual facets of being. It was a time of profound personal journeying into the realm of consciousness medicine. I applied what I had gleaned from my studies, adhering to the principle of 'do no harm' while trusting in the process of spontaneous or self-healing. Drawing upon wisdom from Eastern practices and ancient philosophies, the emphasis was always on the role of the mind and consciousness. At that particular time and place, I was a pioneer in this work, carving a new path through the landscape of healing support practice and self-discovery.

This transformative period was marked by a harmonious blend of teachings from the Monroe Institute, HeartMath Institute, NLP, neuroscience, and neurofeedback, alongside principles from nutrient-rich protocols like the Gerson protocol and functional medicine. It was the integration of holistic medicine with psycho-spiritual elements that truly set us apart. By creating an environment that encouraged the innate intelligence within each participant, we were able to unlock the healing wisdom of the non-ordinary state of mind. Breathwork, movement, intentional thinking, and mindset training were our tools, eliminating the need for any consciousness-altering substances.

The experience was profoundly beautiful and transformative. We witnessed peaceful transitions and healing among participants, whose ages ranged from as young as 3 to our eldest participant at 82. Unburdened by fear and pain, these individuals embarked on a journey of self-discovery and healing.

A unique feature of our retreat was the inclusion of "boot camps." These sessions served as intensive training for the mind, using sound, rhythm, music, and guided visualizations to transport the participants to spaces beyond their ordinary routines. These 'boot camps' were eagerly anticipated and culminated in expressions of heartfelt gratitude towards one another. We witnessed firsthand the potent healing power of love, gratitude, and present-moment awareness—demonstrating that they are, indeed, powerful forms of medicine.

The ability to extend deadlines has been gleaned from my observations across diverse disciplines. These include darkness retreats, lifestyle medicine that incorporates comprehensive changes to lifestyle, diet, environment, thought patterns, daily activities, indigenous plant medicine retreats, and medical qigong. These experiences span various eras, from the works of Edgar Cayce during the New Age era to contemporary practitioners like Dr. Stanislav Grof.

The rich tapestry of evidence supporting these practices is vast and multi-faceted. Each discipline, in its unique way, contributes to the transformative power of healing that I've witnessed in my participants. This amalgamation of insights has taught me that the capacity to extend the deadline isn't merely wishful thinking, but a reality that can be achieved through an integrative, holistic approach to healing.

The underlying thread that ties these diverse experiences together is the human capacity for change.

Whether through a change in mindset, lifestyle, or the way we relate to our bodies, these shifts pave the way for profound healing and extending the so-called 'deadline.' This powerful realization continues to shape my approach to healthcare and healing, instilling in me an unshakeable belief in the potential for transformation in each one of us.

I have witnessed, first-hand, many instances which illustrate the transformative power of the mind-body-spirit connection. Out of respect for their privacy, I will change the names of my participants, but the details of their cases will remain the same.

Stephanie was a 42-year-old woman who came to us with terminal-stage liver cancer. Given just 1-2 months to live by her doctors, she sought an alternative path to managing her condition. After immersing herself in the teachings of our retreat, Stephanie was able to extend her lifespan considerably, passing away peacefully eight months later, far exceeding her initial prognosis.

Mark was a 65-year-old man with terminal brain cancer. His prognosis was similarly grim, with doctors predicting only six months left. Like Stephanie, Mark found a sanctuary in our retreat, practicing mindfulness and integrating the teachings into his daily life. Not only did Mark manage to extend his lifespan, but he also lived those extended two years in peace and comfort.

Nop, an 88-year-old male with colon cancer, was another participant who managed to defy his initial prognosis. Through diligent practice of meditation and lifestyle shifts learned at our retreat, Nop lived many years beyond his predicted deadline. He passed peacefully at home, a testament to the power of mindfulness and lifestyle changes in managing chronic conditions.

Tammy, a 38-year-old woman, came to us with chronic autoimmunity and lifelong sensitivities. She had a history of severe reactions to food, water, and air, conditions that had plagued her for approximately 15 years. After participating in our retreat, Tammy experienced a remarkable recovery. No longer did she exhibit sickly reactions to her environmental triggers. We followed up with her a decade later and were pleased to find that her health had been sustained. Her transformation truly showcased the potential for healing when the mind, body, and spirit are in harmony.

Each of these individuals extended their prognosis not just in terms of lifespan, but also in terms of quality of life. They found comfort, peace, and healing, reinforcing my belief in the profound power of psychospiritual medicine.

During the rise of digital medicine, we were able to leverage advancements in technology to help facilitate healing through lifestyle changes. This led to the creation of a digital lifestyle protocol we called WENA, an acronym for Wellness Expert Navigation System.

WENA was a program that focused on holistic health and wellness, and it was composed of nine carefully designed components, each playing a significant role in a person's overall well-being. These components were structured in a way to not only cover the physical needs of a person but also touch upon their mental, emotional, and social health. The components were as follows:

Food – This component was centered on the importance of nutrition and nourishment, focusing on the quality and variety of food consumed to ensure a well-rounded and balanced diet.

Drink – This area emphasized the necessity of staying hydrated, promoting a healthy intake of water and other beneficial liquids that help regulate bodily functions.

Movement – Recognizing the need for regular physical activity, this component encouraged participants to engage in exercises, sports, and other forms of movement that could stimulate both the body and the mind.

Mind – This section dealt with our mental processes, including our thinking patterns, attitudes, and perspectives. The goal was to foster a positive mindset and promote emotional well-being.

Wear – This component explored the relationship between our clothing and our wellness. It advocated for wearing comfortable and suitable attire, recognizing that what we wear can influence our physical comfort and psychological well-being. The effects of this component will only be felt more deeply with the rise of wearable tech —sensors which constantly monitor biometric data like sleep, heart rate, blood sugar level, etc.

Space – This section focused on the significance of our environment, from our homes and workplaces to any other spaces we frequently occupied. The aim was to create spaces that fostered peace, productivity, and wellness.

Rest – Acknowledging rest as a crucial factor for health, healing, and well-being, this component stressed the importance of good quality sleep, as it is often considered one of the best forms of medicine.

Self-care – This part underscored the need for self-care and self-love, encouraging participants to take time to engage in activities that nourish their soul and make them feel rejuvenated.

Social & Spiritual – Lastly, this component focused on the essential aspects of our social connections and spiritual awareness. It fostered an understanding of the role these connections play in our happiness and overall sense of belonging in the world.

Among the many participants at the retreat center was a young woman, just 42, who was grappling with the advanced stages of liver cancer. This particular cancer is notorious for its aggressive spread and systemic impact, making it all the more difficult for her. The disease had rendered her weak and in constant pain. She had traveled all the way from Chicago, accompanied by her devoted husband, to participate in our Medical Qigong program. They had committed to a two-week retreat with the intention to learn and carry the healing protocol back home.

The protocol involved learning the classical Medical Qigong meditation, which guided participants through visualizations underscored by soothing music and rhythm. This practice was designed to coax the mind into an extraordinary state, capable of reshaping the beliefs and patterns manifesting in the physical body. At the time, the science behind this practice was still a bit of a mystery to me. However, I had seen its potency through numerous instances of spontaneous healing. It's fascinating how this approach echoed the cancer program at the Monroe Institute, popularly referred to as the "journey to T-cells." This program, like ours, utilized guided visualizations to access our extraordinary states of mind and reprogram our physical bodies to generate immune cells, or "T-cells." Through further research and exploration of psychedelic studies, I began to understand our inherent ability to reset, restore, and activate the inner healing intelligence within us.

To truly unlock this inner healing intelligence, a proper set and setting is needed when we venture into an extraordinary state of mind. It involves surrender, a letting go, allowing this intelligence to work its healing magic. When the couple returned home, the woman was in a more peaceful state of mind. Her pain, stress, and anxiety had visibly lessened. We maintained regular contact until her peaceful passing, surrounded by her loved ones. Her husband was grateful for the two weeks they spent at the Medical Qigong retreat, stating how the experience had significantly eased her transition and empowered the family to navigate their circumstances more effectively.

Life's expiration date remains one of its greatest enigmas, shrouded in uncertainty and mystery. As long as we breathe, our focus should be to cultivate joy in the present moment, fulfill our life's purpose, and acknowledge that we're here to experience, explore, and express ourselves fully. With the right mindset and a heart brimming with gratitude, we hold the keys to craft a beautiful, joyous life.

Extraordinary states of consciousness play an instrumental role in enabling lifestyle changes. Implementing change in our lives often presents a challenge, as our pre-existing paradigms and patterns are deeply ingrained, cultivating a resistance to flexibility and change. We are naturally inclined to traverse the path of least resistance, adhering to routines that foster comfort and ease. However, when we face resistance and attempt to counter the established flow without clear objectives or persistent effort, inducing change becomes an uphill battle in our current state of consciousness.

Albert Einstein insightfully noted, "no problem can be solved from the same level of consciousness that created it." This rings especially true when we find ourselves ensnared in life's painful and bewildering experiences, where the world seems steeped in chaos, and we feel trapped. This principle isn't limited to simple lifestyle modifications but applies to the full spectrum of complexities in life.

Extraordinary states of consciousness offer us a transformative gateway, enabling a shift in perspective and emancipating us from the constraints of habitual thinking. We can access these extraordinary states through various means—meditation, breathwork, psychedelic experiences, or other practices designed to expand our consciousness. By transcending our ordinary states, we open ourselves to new insights, heightened awareness, and a novel understanding of our own selves and our environment.

In these extraordinary states, our perception of reality undergoes a metamorphosis, revealing previously obscured possibilities and solutions. We can tap into our intuition, form a connection with our inner wisdom, and access profound states conducive to healing and growth. These states serve as fertile ground for exploration, empowering us to make enlightened choices and embrace positive lifestyle modifications.

By embracing an expansion of our consciousness and delving into extraordinary states of mind, we unlock a treasure trove of new perspectives, insights, and transformative experiences. We can shatter the constraints of our previous patterns, surmount resistance to change, and embark on a journey toward personal evolution. The embrace of these extraordinary states of consciousness serves as a catalyst for positive growth, aiding us in navigating life's challenges, making informed choices, and leading a more fulfilling and purposeful existence.

This notion isn't novel. Several notable thinkers, innovators, and pioneers throughout history have reported gaining significant insights and breakthroughs while in non-ordinary states of mind. Steve Jobs, Thomas Edison, Albert Hofmann, Carl Jung, Robert Monroe, among others, have all touted the transformative potential of these extraordinary states, serving as a testament to their power in shaping the trajectory of individual lives and humanity at large.

Of course, the psycho-spiritual approach to life is not a ticket to eternity on Earth. At a recent psychedelic science conference, one of the largest in the USA, I was confronted with the somber reality that some of the pioneering scientists and psychedelic explorers may not be present at future events due to their dire prognoses.

In addressing the extension of life, it is crucial to recognize and honor the reality that not all lives can be extended. To imply otherwise could sow false hopes, potentially causing emotional harm. We must be prepared, emotionally and mentally, for the inevitable conclusion of our mortal journey, whenever it may come.

As the shadow of mortality looms large, our psychological processes must often navigate grief. Prominent psychiatrist Dr. Elisabeth Kubler-Ross developed a model of grief that delineates the psychological process as consisting of five stages: denial, anger, bargaining, depression, and ultimately, acceptance. This process is often seen as a protective mechanism of the human psyche in response to loss or significant life changes. Yet navigating through these stages can be emotionally taxing.

However, I stand by the belief that not everyone necessarily needs to tread through all these stages. With enlightenment or a profound understanding of the mind's intricacies, it's feasible to blend, truncate, or even bypass the conventional stages of grief. When one is genuinely aware and knowledgeable about their own psyche, this provides a pathway to mitigate the often arduous journey of grieving.

By welcoming this enlightened perspective, individuals may chart a different and perhaps more efficient path toward healing and acceptance. This viewpoint doesn't negate the depth or legitimacy of their pain; rather, it offers a way to navigate through it with a greater sense of understanding and compassion. By recognizing the universality of suffering and loss, we can approach our pain with tenderness, allowing ourselves to fully experience it without being overwhelmed by it.

In the grand tapestry of existence, the threads of joy and sorrow are woven together, each one contributing to the rich, complex patterns that define our lives. In understanding this, we can embrace each moment, whether it brings happiness or grief, as a precious part of our journey. Through this acceptance, we can navigate life's inevitable challenges with grace, resilience, and wisdom, honoring our experiences, and cherishing our ability to grow through them.

As we conclude this chapter, let us take a moment to appreciate the profound interconnectedness of life and death, joy and sorrow, health and sickness. Let us remember that every stage of our journey offers invaluable lessons and opportunities for growth. And above all, let us cherish the gift of existence, with all its complexities and contradictions, for it is in embracing this holistic perspective that we can truly both live and die well.

Gratitude and Psychedelics

The power of gratitude has been as impactful for me as the visions and enlightenment offered by psychedelic experiences. As a guiding light in my life, its effects have been both anchor and catalyst, grounding me during times of adversity and propelling me into realms of personal and spiritual growth. This transformative feeling has not just been a situational antidote but a theme that recurs and evolves, enabling me to continuously reinvent myself and manifest abundance on multiple planes of existence. From the ethereal joys that life offers to the concrete milestones in my entrepreneurial journey, this transformative feeling has been the driving force behind it all.

It took me nearly three decades of personal exploration, from early meditation practices to immersive experiences at institutions like the Monroe Institute and practitioner training at the HeartMath Institute, to fully grasp the profound depths of gratitude.

HeartMath's approach highlights the heart's influential electromagnetic field and its impact on emotions and well-being. When combined with mindfulness and psychedelic-assisted psychotherapy, HeartMath can enhance therapeutic outcomes and facilitate personal growth.

As the first certified HeartMath professional, I've explored the intricate relationship between the heart and mind, focusing on stress management and heart coherence. I've coached diverse clients—from restless kindergarteners and rebellious teenagers to stressed-out CEOs and individuals with declining health—to build resilience and manage stress.

From original techniques like "Freeze-Frame" and "Heart Lock-In" to newer methods like "Heart Resilience," HeartMath has proven effective for people of all ages and backgrounds.

My relationship with gratitude is cemented through daily practices. Each morning and evening, taking the time to engage with this transformative feeling is as routine to me as brushing my teeth. These quiet moments set the tone for the day ahead and offer a reflection of the day that has passed. But my practice extends beyond these dedicated times. As I navigate the various circumstances and challenges of everyday life, I consciously shift into this state of transformation. gratitude is not just a passive acknowledgment but an active tool that I deploy to manage life's complexities.

Each moment of my life is an opportunity to engage with this powerful consciousness. It's not just about acknowledging what I have, but also about leveraging this sense to manifest what I desire—while taking the necessary actions to make it a reality. This serves as my internal compass, guiding my actions and decisions, and thereby, enriching my life and those around me.

Whether it's through daily affirmations, conscious efforts during life's trials, or even through spiritual and scientific explorations, gratitude remains my steadfast companion. It serves as both a grounding mechanism and a launching pad, ever-present in its ability to transform and enlighten every facet of my existence.

During transitional phases, life often demands that we lean into faith and trust. For me, gratitude has served as the ever-reliable fuel that powers these invaluable virtues. It is a refuge that holds me steady during tumultuous times. Living in the present moment, absent of fear and worry, becomes possible when the frequency of gratitude vibrates within me. I dedicate hours each day, morning and night, to this practice. As I write down what I am grateful for, I can feel myself resonating at that frequency —often culminating in a state of joy, happiness, and bliss.

But, enough about me. Let's zoom out a bit and take a look at gratitude from a broader, societal perspective.

It is both a cognitive and emotional experience that profoundly shapes our thoughts and actions. When we take the time to express gratitude, we are engaging in an act of mindfulness, pulling ourselves back to recognize the richness of our lives. This act of recognition changes the frequency of our energy, helping us shift from a state of contraction, where negative thoughts prevail, to one of expansion filled with positive thoughts.

The ripple effects of gratitude are multifaceted. It not only enhances our perception of positive experiences but also broadens our perspective, diminishing our natural inclination toward negative bias. By recalibrating our thought processes through the lens of gratitude, we find ourselves capable of reframing deeply-rooted beliefs and enhancing our sense of self-worth. This, in turn, amplifies our resilience and capacity to overcome life's many challenges.

In addition to its biochemical effects, gratitude fundamentally shifts our mental focus. Instead of fixating on what we lack, gratitude tunes our attention to what we already have, effectively reducing the "noise" of our incessant thoughts and concerns. This acts like an anchor, grounding us in the present moment, and creating a sanctuary of mental peace.

Despite its reputation as an abstract or lofty emotion, gratitude has very real, measurable impacts on physical health. An expanding body of research attests to this, demonstrating the various ways in which cultivating gratitude can improve our physiological well-being. From strengthening immune responses to promoting cardiovascular health, the effects of gratitude on the body are multifaceted.

One significant benefit of gratitude is its ability to boost the immune system. Those who frequently practice gratitude report fewer health complaints and stronger immune responses. Cardiovascular health is another area positively influenced by gratitude, with improved heart rate variability and reduced blood pressure among the reported benefits.

When you sum it all up, what we are talking about here

is the act of extending life itself. A regular practice of gratitude is associated with a healthier lifestyle, which can contribute to a longer, more fulfilling life.

The emotional benefits of gratitude are not just anecdotal but backed by neuroscience. This simple act stimulates the production of neurotransmitters like dopamine and serotonin, which are intimately connected with our moods, emotions, and feelings of pleasure. Dopamine and serotonin have been mentioned in quite a few chapters of this book, and with good reason. They're often dubbed the "feel-good" neurotransmitters and are essential for feelings of happiness and general well-being. The frequency with which we practice gratitude can play a pivotal role in shifting our state of consciousness. It's as though gratitude serves as a natural antidote, chemically balancing our brains to alleviate symptoms of mental disorders and improve our overall emotional health. These biochemical changes can elevate our awareness and lead us to a heightened state of tranquility. What's particularly fascinating is that emotions like gratitude have been linked to more harmonious and coherent brainwave activity.

Neuroscience has been making significant strides in understanding how gratitude physically alters our brain structure and chemistry. One of the key regions implicated in the process is the medial prefrontal cortex (mPFC), a part of the brain crucial for cognitive processing, emotional regulation, motivation, and sociability. The mPFC serves as a sort of neural hub, integrating information from various input structures in the brain and updating it before sending it out to output structures. Interestingly, dysfunction in the mPFC has been correlated with a host of neurological and psychological disorders like depression, anxiety, schizophrenia, autism, Alzheimer's, Parkinson's, and even addiction.

Then there's the amygdala, the part of the brain often referred to as our emotional sentinel. It plays a major role in processing emotions, particularly those associated with threat detection. Practicing gratitude has been shown to reduce reactivity in the amygdala, effectively dampening our physiological stress responses. The amygdala also plays a significant role in forming emotionally-laden memories. When we have intense emotional experiences—whether they are instances of profound gratitude or deeply traumatic events—the amygdala stores these experiences in a particularly resonant way.

The emerging field of neuroscience thus confirms what many have long suspected: gratitude isn't just a social nicety or a spiritual axiom; it's a potent instrument for positive change, with measurable effects on our brain's architecture and chemistry.

Despite these growing mounds of evidence favoring the benefits of gratitude, we live in a world where not everyone practices it. The pace and demands of modern living often push us toward states of suffering, disappointment, frustration, anger, and sadness. The relentless demands for perfection, for more and yet more, often lead to emotional and psychological strain.

Before I fully embraced the practice of gratitude, I too suffered when I overreached, trying to do too much and ending up disappointed. However, when I learned to trust that we are all part of a greater whole and that this whole supports us, the very nature of my life changed. It began to move in directions I never thought possible, all guided by my deep-rooted sense of gratitude.

Gratitude is far more than a simple "thank you"; it's a powerful emotion that has been revered across cultures and traditions as a transformative tool. When one dives into the depths of gratitude, genuinely feeling it in every fiber of their being, there's a palpable shift in mental state.

There are many facets to this practice of thankfulness. We can think of it as a tree. It will grow if we give it daylight—meaning practice it regularly. It bears fruits that benefit not only us, but our surroundings. Its roots spread into every corner of our lives, but of all these aspects of this imaginary tree, there is one vibrant element with beauty that cannot be understated—its flowers.

Also known as: kindness.

There is a symbiotic relationship between gratitude and kindness; each amplifies the other. Expressing gratitude can serve as the spark for acts of kindness, and acts of kindness can feed back into our sense of gratitude. This creates a virtuous cycle, strengthening our belief in the value of reciprocity in human relationships, whether we are aware of it or not.

Kindness is not just a fleeting emotional state; it is a fundamental human value that permeates our existence, shapes our interactions, and contributes to the universal fabric of well-being. Just as everything in the universe is in a constant state of vibration, so too does kindness resonate through us with its unique frequency. This frequency doesn't exist in isolation; it is part of a greater universal orchestra. Each one of us contributes to this celestial music through the emotional and vibrational frequency we emit.

What's fascinating is the symbiotic relationship between these two states. When two frequencies, like gratitude and kindness, resonate with each other, they have the potential to synchronize. This synchronization leads to a sort of spontaneous self-organization, where each state amplifies and enhances the other. But this is not a straightforward process; there can be a period of dissonance, a "chaos period," before the frequencies align and harmony is achieved.

Gratitude has a significant role in the normative regulation of social relationships. It fosters key human qualities like generosity, trust, and humility, contributing to both individual and collective well-being. In the modern world, as we navigate the complexities of human interactions and societal pressures, the timeless and universal practice of gratitude stands as a potent tool for personal and communal transformation.

Now, how does all of this relate to the popular topic of psychedelics?

As I mentioned, gratitude triggers the release of dopamine and serotonin. Intriguingly, similar biochemical processes are observed in psychedelic states, which are also known to facilitate profound feelings of interconnectedness and gratitude. Both the practice of gratitude and the use of psychedelics can mitigate stress by reducing stress hormone levels and recalibrating the brain's stress responses. This could potentially have applications in pain management, where both states—gratitude and psychedelics—have been shown to alter pain perception.

I've observed that the heightened state of consciousness achieved through gratitude can align with the frequencies reached during psychedelic experiences, offering a different layer of awareness or level of consciousness altogether.

In the sphere of extraordinary human experiences, both profound gratitude and psychedelic states occupy significant space. In many ways, being in a state of deep, transpersonal gratitude can feel akin to a mild psychedelic experience. I often describe this level of gratitude as the emotional equivalent of micro-dosing on psychedelics.

Both gratitude and psychedelics serve as catalysts for transformative experiences, and—like the interplay between gratitude and kindness—their effects can be synergistic. In my own journey, I've found that intense feelings of gratitude can actually induce psychedelic experiences. Conversely, a psychedelic state of mind can deepen one's sense of gratitude and connectedness to the world. This creates a fascinating loop of causality between the two, each enriching and amplifying the other's impact.

It's as though gratitude and psychedelics are two sides of the same coin, each providing a unique yet complementary path to transcendental states of mind and emotional well-being. While one is rooted in the world of the everyday and the other often seen as extraordinary, both offer profound opportunities for transformation, connection, and the realization of a more harmonious existence.

To recap what we've learned about psychedelics: When embarking on a journey of this nature, two crucial factors come into play: set and setting. The 'set' refers to your mindset, attitude, intentions, and overall state of mind, while the 'setting' encompasses external factors such as the environment, facilitators, location, and the type of psychedelic medicine involved.

As far as the "mindset" aspect of this duo is concerned, entering into a psychedelic experience with a well-grounded sense of gratitude sets a positive framework that nurtures personal growth, healing, and enlightenment.

Psychedelics also have the fascinating ability to dissolve the ego temporarily, blurring the lines between self and others, which can culminate in a feeling of unity and interconnectedness with all of existence. This naturally evokes profound gratitude, adding another layer to the symbiotic relationship between the two.

In a therapeutic context, psychedelics have been instrumental in healing emotional and traumatic wounds, renewing one's appreciation for life and its fleeting moments. Many who have undergone psychedelic experiences report intense feelings of thankfulness, not just toward specific loved ones but toward life itself.

Therefore, for those considering a psychedelic experience, cultivating a state of gratitude beforehand can have tangible benefits. It creates a positive, emotionally grounded state of mind that can enhance the likelihood of favorable outcomes. The interaction between gratitude and psychedelics seems to be a deeply synergistic dance; each enriches the other, enhancing the depth and meaningfulness of both experiences.

So, whether through the lens of psychedelics or through the practice of gratitude, the outcome is often the same: a dissolution of the ego, a feeling of connectedness, and a sense of unity that deepens our relationships with others and the world. Both avenues offer a path to transcend the self and unite us with something much larger, imbuing us with a sense of significance and purpose within the vast panorama of existence.

Gratitude serves as a significant moral and social regulator, shaping our relationships with others and extending its influence to higher planes of existence, be it the divine, a higher self, or the universe at large. This is remarkably akin to the concept of ego dissolution, where the sense of self begins to fade, and we find ourselves a part of a larger tapestry of existence. Gratitude nudges us outside the boundaries of our individual selves and into a larger, interconnected context that transcends the personal realm.

Reaching a state beyond the personal, we connect not just with other humans but also with the world as a whole. This state of awareness makes us feel simultaneously tiny within the vast scope of the universe and yet incredibly significant to be a part of it all. It enhances our awareness and fosters a stronger bond with everything around us, transcending the mere human-to-human connection.

The concept of connectedness revolves around the

feeling of being intrinsically linked to others while still maintaining a sense of individuality. It's a sensation of being part of something far greater than oneself. This experience of connectedness often occurs during deeply transpersonal moments filled with heartfelt gratitude, as well as during psychedelic experiences. The feeling of connectedness is closely related to experiences of unity, reinforcing a sense of belonging, bonding, and inclusivity among individuals.

From a more practical standpoint, gratitude has the power to foster respect between individuals, nurturing relationships and enhancing social cohesion. It acts as a mirror, reflecting our self-awareness and enabling us to acknowledge and appreciate the empathy and care contributed by others. This, in turn, cultivates a harmonious community and environment.

Gratitude is a universal sentiment, but its expression and impact can vary greatly across different cultures and belief systems. In most societies, gratitude is intricately linked with notions of duty, obligation, and social decorum. Acts of generosity often carry an expectation of thankfulness, which in turn fosters moral and social harmony.

However, the gratitude I speak of goes beyond these social norms and expectations; it's about a deeper, more profound form of gratitude that can be described as transpersonal. Yet, to access this higher level of gratitude, one often must start with the basics—simple acts of thankfulness and appreciation that are part and parcel of the human experience.

Gratitude is universal in its essence but varies in its expression and experience across cultures. Whether you're in the East or the West, each culture has its unique way of recognizing, expressing, and celebrating gratitude. Eastern traditions often use non-verbal cues to express emotions and feelings, whereas Western cultures are generally more overt and expressive. In the United States, this is taken all the way to the point of making it a national holiday—Thanksgiving.

Religious and spiritual systems, too, have their own rituals and ceremonies for expressing gratitude. Islam employs prayers and prostrations, Judaism uses blessings, and Buddhism incorporates merit, meditation, rituals, and ceremonies. Hinduism practices gratitude through Puja and ritual offerings, and indigenous cultures express it through their own unique rituals and ceremonies.

It's as if the universe, in its infinite wisdom, has given us this tool of gratitude, which costs nothing but has profound effects on our lives.

Not all expressions of gratitude are created equal. On a basic level, gratitude can be expressed as a form of politeness or social etiquette. This is something every human should engage in as it satisfies basic social needs and obligations. However, at higher levels of conscious awareness, gratitude takes on a more transformative role. Here, it's not about expecting something in return; it's about using gratitude as a tool for personal growth, enlightenment, and living a life without limitations.

Gratitude is a multi-layered experience. While it starts with basic social interactions and common courtesies, it can evolve into a deep, profound, transpersonal state. As we mature in our understanding and practice of gratitude, it becomes less about social expectations and more about personal and spiritual growth. This transformative power of gratitude is universally available to all of us, and understanding this can open doors to living life in its fullest, most joyous state.

Despite hearing about its importance from a multitude of teachers and mentors over the years, it wasn't until I delved into the science of heart signaling frequencies and vibrations that I truly understood its power. As Eastern practices suggest, the heart can be considered a 'second mind,' with the gut as the 'third mind,' each having its unique influence alongside the cognitive brain. For me, gratitude activates these multiple 'minds,' creating a symphony of positive energy and clarity.

I consider myself blessed to have been mentored by such luminaries as Mary Morrissey and the late Bob Proctor. Their teachings were instrumental in embedding gratitude as the cornerstone of my life. During my weekly virtual study sessions in Bob's inner circle, we dived deep into some life-altering texts, such as Wallace Wattles' 1910 work, "The Science of Being Great," particularly its seventh chapter on gratitude. The beauty of this practice lay not just in reading but in becoming one with the thoughts of the author. The idea was to read, reread, and delve so deeply into the text that the distinctions between the author's thoughts and my own would blur. This was not about acquisition but about transformation.

In my years of coaching using the HeartMath™ system,

I've seen the transformative power of gratitude firsthand. This approach focuses on shifting attention, cultivating a resilient mind, and transforming an anxious state into one of coherence. One of the techniques involves centering attention on the heart, re-experiencing gratitude, joy, and happiness, and thereby maintaining a state of homeostasis. Even in stressful situations, we can become aware of our emotional state and realign it with the resonance of gratitude, significantly reducing stress, anxiety, and fear. It's a profound state of being, and I can honestly say that I am in bliss most of the time.

In every conversation, whether it's with friends, mentors, community leaders, or elders, the common thread is the practice of gratitude. Even in my interactions with experts at the Psychedelic Science Conference—like Dr. Richard Louis Miller, Rick Doblin, Alex and Allyson Gray, Dennis McKenna, and Adam Bramlage—gratitude is a constant.

Imagine a world infused with enhanced levels of gratitude, a world that is as transformative and expansive as a psychedelic experience. Such a world would be a vibrant tapestry of love, compassion, kindness, and abundance. My recent involvement in the first cohort on Psychedelic Assisted Therapy (PAT), hosted by the Multidisciplinary Association for Psychedelic Studies (MAPS) and Monash University in Australia, exemplifies this vision. Our small community – physicians, psychiatrists, psychologists, psychotherapists, nurses, and other healthcare practitioners – teemed with love, empathy, and, most of all, gratitude. That's right: all 60 of us actively practiced gratitude! I know that this is not mere coincidence. This micro-community serves as a prototype for the potential macro-society—a society founded on collective consciousness and grateful interconnectedness.

This unifying thread in the psychedelic community, driven by heart-centeredness, gratitude, and a focus on serving humanity, leaves me humbled. We are in an extraordinary period, healing humanity through the powerful interplay of gratitude and psychedelic experiences.

Similar sentiments echo in other communities I'm part of —like Abundance 360, led by Peter Diamandis, or my brave-thinking master class guided by Mary Morrissey. Whether it's HeartMath Institute, the Monroe Institute, or various other communities led by thought leaders like Dr. David Morehouse, Dr. Richard Louis Miller, and Dr. Rick Doblin, the practice of deep, meaningful gratitude is a constant.

Gratitude has a magnetic quality; it attracts more of itself. Surrounding myself with communities steeped in gratitude has had a catalytic effect, transforming not just my life but also imprinting on the collective consciousness. From religious and spiritual figures like the Dalai Lama to everyday people, the practice of loving-kindness—another form of gratitude—is contagious. Imagine the transformative power of such an emotional state if practiced globally, one village at a time.

Gratitude, in my experience, is a constant, unwavering force that has never let me down. Its very essence seems to function as a magnet, attracting more and more of the same quality into my life. The principle is simple yet profound: We are made of a "thinking substance," and this thinking substance takes on the form of what it contemplates. A mind filled with gratitude naturally attracts circumstances that resonate with that sense of thankfulness. This has led me to develop a method of communicating with my own consciousness through the lens of gratitude, creating a life abundant in happiness and fulfillment.

As I pen this, my heart swells with contentment, a testament to the frequency of gratitude that I now live by. If you're reading this, know that my intention is for the resonance of gratitude within me to touch you, offering you a glimpse into this powerful emotional state that has the potential to enrich every aspect of our lives. Whenever I close my eyes, I am enveloped in a bliss of gratitude, and my heart feels full and content. That is the power and beauty of living a life attuned to the frequency of gratitude.

It's remarkable how this fascinating power has caught me by surprise, particularly during times when I saw no way forward. Yet, there always turned out to be a way— often in the most unexpected, even miraculous, forms. This is the clarity and focus that comes from living in a constant state of gratitude.

This state is a practical tool for manifesting desired outcomes. By expressing gratitude for future events, I've found that those events often come to fruition, sooner or later. Even when faced with negative or challenging circumstances, finding the silver lining and expressing gratitude for it has an almost instant transformative effect.

One could say that gratitude has been my secret weapon for navigating the various challenges life throws my way. Whether it's finding a parking space when I'm running late or diffusing potentially life-threatening conflicts, the energy of gratitude has offered peaceful and sometimes even miraculous solutions.

Traditionally, gratitude has been associated with thankfulness and often considered an obligation or a virtue, both socially and spiritually. (For example, how many of our cultures teach us to say 'Thank you' when we are just beginning to talk?). However, as our understanding of gratitude evolves, we come to see it as more than just a moral or ethical choice. When gratitude is expressed deeply and without the expectation of something in return, it transcends the social and the spiritual to provide a sense of fulfillment.

While everyone is inherently capable of experiencing and expressing gratitude, achieving a deep, transpersonal level of it often requires more than just intent—it requires guidance and regular practice. Some individuals even experience life-altering events that catapult them into states of profound gratitude. Unlike the second-hand understanding one may gain from reading a book or watching a movie, true gratitude needs to be personally experienced for its depth to be fully understood.

Several factors contribute to a person's ability to express gratitude, from their mindset and attitude to their upbringing, environment, and even genetic makeup. The good news is that many of these elements can be adjusted or shifted to enhance one's capability for spontaneous and pure expressions of gratitude. By maintaining a proper mindset and attitude, individuals can access various levels of gratitude, from everyday thankfulness to transformative, transpersonal gratitude.

Throughout history, humankind has oscillated between periods of constructive and destructive behaviors, often driven by a complex interplay of cultural, societal, and emotional factors. Gratitude plays a crucial role in both cycles. During constructive phases, a mindset of gratitude can heighten creativity. During destructive cycles, gratitude becomes even more important for breaking negative patterns and facilitating non-violent conflict resolution.

Gratitude allows us to tap into our innate capacity to build and rebuild, design and redesign. This makes it a cornerstone for societal advancement. Far from being limited by our immediate circumstances or mindset, gratitude empowers us to explore our unlimited potential, enriching both the individual and the collective human experience.

Simply put, gratitude is a transformative force, as powerful as any technology or idea mankind has ever seen. It's not merely something we feel but something we practice, share, and spread—like a joyful contagion that has the power to reshape the world, one thankful thought at a time.

The transformative power of gratitude cannot be understated. By earnestly practicing gratitude, we can dramatically alter our emotional landscape, shifting from negative to positive thought patterns. However, it's important to note that this transformation isn't instantaneous; it requires discipline and a willingness to deeply engage with one's own emotional terrain.

So, the next time you take a moment to give thanks, remember that the act does far more than merely acknowledging a good deed or a fortunate circumstance—it physically alters the building blocks of your thoughts and emotions.

Psychedelic-Assisted Therapy

In an era where the collective consciousness seems increasingly attuned to the quest for growth and transformation, there has never been a more exhilarating time to be alive. Whether it's the global community at large or perhaps the like-minded individuals I've consciously surrounded myself with, I observe a growing consensus around the need for unified action aimed at healing humanity and elevating our collective spiritual and emotional well-being. This thirst for transformative change dovetails remarkably well with advancements on various fronts of mental health research and practice.

Among these advancements, one area that stands out for its transformative potential is the realm of psychedelic therapy. Particularly noteworthy is the emerging field of MDMA-assisted therapy, which is showing significant promise for the treatment of Post-Traumatic Stress Disorder (PTSD) and psilocybin-assisted therapy for severe depression. The unfolding work in this area can be likened to "cracking the psychedelic code," a revolutionary breakthrough that is expanding the horizons of healing beyond the scope of conventional methods. Among the myriad possibilities that this newfound understanding of psychedelics opens up, its potential to offer relief and lasting recovery for those grappling with PTSD is one of its most extraordinary promises.

Understanding PTSD requires a look back through the annals of medical history and the various phases of our evolving knowledge of mental health disorders. What began as "shell-shock"—a term coined to describe the psychological torment faced by soldiers during World War I—has, through years of study and refined diagnostic criteria, evolved into what we now recognize as PTSD. This complex and often debilitating condition can be triggered by a wide array of traumatic experiences. The triggers for PTSD are as varied as they are distressing: the brutalities of combat, physical or sexual assault, natural disasters, and the psychological toll of difficult relationships or childhood trauma.

In its intricacy, PTSD is not just the result of external events but also stems from a complex interplay of underlying psychological, physiological, and environmental factors. The paths leading to PTSD are multifaceted and intertwined with various underlying factors.

Just as the intricacies of PTSD defy simple explanations, so, too, does the path to treating it. Over half a century ago, significant progress in its treatment seemed almost within reach. Yet, societal factors forced us down a detour, especially when it came to the role of psychedelics. During the 1960s, substances like LSD and psilocybin burgeoned in popularity, not merely as recreational drugs but as gateways to self-discovery, spiritual enlightenment, and even political activism. Unfortunately, this wave of interest in the therapeutic potential of psychedelics also led to societal backlash, putting us at a crossroads that lengthened the journey to understanding their medicinal value.

The era was a tableau of contrasting themes, with the Vietnam War casting a dark cloud even as people sought peace, love, and understanding. At this nexus of war, love, and psychedelic exploration, societal shifts occurred. The anti-war movement's call for love and empathy resonated in the arts and in the quest for altered states of consciousness. In a similar vein, the devastating impacts of war made the healing potentials of psychedelic substances more appealing.

The 1960s were not just about peace, protests, and psychedelic trips. The era was also marked by a flourishing of human connection and love, giving rise to the "flower power" movement. Far from a mere cultural fad, this was a transformative period that stressed the interconnectedness of all beings, the virtue of compassion, and a focus on both personal and societal betterment. Yet, the purity of these ideals was compromised. Driven by a volatile combination of political activism, psychedelic use, and revolutionary fervor, the true essence of love became distorted, sometimes for manipulative or greedy ends.

This entanglement of love with politics and substances led to a period of disillusionment. The potential for psychedelics to serve as tools for deeper human connection was sidetracked by abuses and misunderstandings. What began as a noble endeavor to understand the self and the other devolved at times into a maze of excessive idealism and societal complexities.

My own connection to this era is one that reaches across time, by way of cultural echoes. Back in the late 80s, when I was working with refugees on the Thai-Cambodia border, I was struck by the palpable echoes of the 1960s. In this far-removed setting, the cultural memory seemed to hang suspended in that transformative decade. The melodies of the Beatles and other iconic '60s artists filled the air, merging seamlessly with the atmosphere of change and exploration that characterized the era. This experience served as both a symbol and a living manifestation of the 1960s' complex web of struggles, aspirations, and ideals. It was as if this decade, often portrayed as a distant relic of history, continued to breathe life into the most unexpected places.

The cultural shifts that erupted during the 1960s had a truly global impact, extending far beyond the countercultural movement of the Western world. The yearning for peace, the bold exploration of psychedelics, and the relentless pursuit of love were not isolated phenomena. They have shaped and influenced various cultures and settings, emphasizing their universal power to transcend both geographical and societal boundaries.

During my time at the camp, as I pondered my personal experiences and their resonance with that epoch, I saw the 1960s not just as a period of history but as a living philosophy. The ideals of that time continue to reverberate through new generations, shaping our individual and collective trajectories.

The "War on Drugs" acts as a pivotal chapter in the meandering history of psychedelics, effectively creating a roadblock on what was already a winding path to understanding their therapeutic potential. Rooted in a turbulent period of cultural and political change, this war stemmed from a reactive, often punitive stance by the government. While the 1960s counterculture movement celebrated personal freedom and spiritual enlightenment through psychedelics, the government's aggressive response put the brakes on this exploratory journey. Sensationalized media and public fear, fueled by misuse and abuse of these substances, led to stringent legal measures that not only criminalized usage but also stunted scientific inquiry and therapeutic applications.

As my previous discussion elucidated, this era was a crucible for a myriad of competing themes—war, love, and spiritual questing—all of which were complicated by the misuse of psychedelics and the subsequent legislative crackdown. The "War on Drugs" can be seen as an overcorrection, a policy driven more by a punitive approach rather than a nuanced understanding of public health. The effect was essentially to deepen the shadows surrounding psychedelics.

However, just as the narrative around psychedelics has begun to change in recent years, so too has the perspective on the drug policies that kept them in the dark. There is a burgeoning consensus advocating for a pivot in strategy, one rooted in evidence-based approaches and harm-reduction. A shift from punishment to prevention could serve as the cornerstone of a more enlightened, effective policy. This modern understanding acknowledges the multifaceted nature of drug use, considering social, economic, and psychological factors, and potentially clearing the path for psychedelics to reclaim their lost therapeutic promise.

Thus, the "War on Drugs" not only serves as a cautionary tale but also as a call for a new paradigm. The lessons of the past, especially those learned during the tumultuous 1960s, are instructive for forging a future where psychedelics can be responsibly integrated into a broader therapeutic context. Despite the missteps and pitfalls, the decade has provided a valuable roadmap for understanding the multifaceted and transcendent nature of love.

This reflection gains special relevance in the context of the resurgence of psychedelic-assisted therapy. The concept of love in this modern therapeutic framework has become far more nuanced, informed by years of research, wisdom, and professional expertise. Here, love is no longer viewed as a transient emotion but as an innate capacity for compassion, connection, and transcendence. We must approach psychedelics with this balanced understanding, honoring both their potential and their risks. By doing so, we not only navigate the present but also pay homage to the psychedelic era, a time that serves as a reminder that the quest for enlightenment, freedom, and healing must be navigated with wisdom, empathy, and responsibility.

In hindsight, the path of psychedelics from their heyday

in the 1960s to the present is a tale of both caution and resurgence. Initial enthusiasm gave way to a prolonged hiatus, marked by legal restrictions that hindered research and perpetuated stigma. But this is not where the story ends. Recent years have seen a renewed interest in these substances, a reawakening that I believe is far from coincidental. It suggests a larger cultural pivot—a readiness to revisit the past with the wisdom of the present, and to treat these substances with the respect and understanding they deserve. Now, the insights gleaned from the mistakes and learnings of the 1960s are catalyzing a new era of responsible, empathic, and healing-focused exploration of psychedelics.

I'm writing this very chapter from the Flowerdale Estate in Australia, participating in the first cohort of MAPS (Multidisciplinary Association for Psychedelic Studies) MDMA-assisted therapy training in Australia, hosted by Monash University. A sense of profound excitement and purpose envelops me. This occasion marks the first training session MAPS has offered since 2017 and is the inaugural event for Australia. It's not just a momentous occasion for me, but a historical one for the nation. Australia has recently distinguished itself as the first country to legalize psychedelic-assisted therapy for PTSD, a milestone that signals a shifting paradigm in mental health treatment. The world is watching, and I can sense that we are on the cusp of an even more groundbreaking path—legalization for Treatment-Resistant Depression is the next frontier.

But what really fuels my enthusiasm is the recognition

that psychedelics are not a one-size-fits-all solution for treating PTSD. The field is broad and dynamic, constantly evolving as new data and research unfold. MDMA and psilocybin, for example, have proven to be particularly potent in different ways. MDMA-assisted therapy, with its predictability and capacity to cultivate empathy and emotional safety, stands as a promising avenue for those seeking relief from the symptoms of PTSD. Meanwhile, psilocybin offers a journey that is more introspective, less predictable, yet incredibly valuable in exploring and processing the depths of one's trauma.

It's not just these two compounds that show promise. Other substances, such as Ibogaine and Ayahuasca, along with techniques like Darkness Retreat and Breathwork, each offer unique therapeutic potentials. As a trauma healing facilitator, I am learning that the key to effective treatment is in personalization—tailoring each approach to align with the patient's specific needs, guided by experienced facilitators. And it is this complexity and dynamism that make the field so incredibly promising. We are still unlocking the secrets to deep-seated healing, and every step we take brings us closer to understanding the intricacies of individual responses to different therapies.

This brings me to the essence of what healing from PTSD truly entails. It is a journey, complicated and deeply personal, and it often involves facing the trauma head-on, albeit within the safety of a guided context. I've found that it's not enough to merely treat the symptoms; we must delve into the very root of the trauma. In my experience, the real transformative work begins when one dares to re-experience the traumatic emotions, allowing oneself to feel them deeply. This dissociates these intense emotions from our psyche and memory, thereby lessening their grip over time. It's an arduous but necessary process. By courageously facing the trauma, we gradually begin to view the traumatic events through a lens of understanding rather than fear.

Reflecting on all of this, I can't help but feel a sense of awe at how far we've come—from the stigmas and legal restrictions that once hindered psychedelic research to a new era marked by acceptance, scientific rigor, and immense potential for healing. It's as if the cultural pivot we are experiencing is not a mere coincidence but a collective readiness to explore the wisdom gleaned from past experiences. And as we move forward, with eyes wide open, we are shaping a future that holds the promise of profound personal and societal transformation.

As we stand at this pivotal moment, reflecting on the intricate dance of love, psychedelics, culture, and healing, it's clear that we're navigating a critical juncture in our collective understanding. The 1960s—an era that defined counterculture and swung open the doors to psychedelic exploration—offered glimpses of potential but also left a trail of misunderstandings and missed opportunities. Today, however, organizations like MAPS are charting a more thoughtful course, supported by a burgeoning body of research.

Our quest goes beyond merely comprehending the therapeutic capabilities of substances like MDMA or psilocybin. It's an exploration that invites us to redefine our notions of love, intimacy, and human connection. It's a call to recognize that genuine healing emanates from a deep well of unconditional love and gratitude. As we responsibly harness the therapeutic power of psychedelics, we are also acknowledging the multifaceted nature of love itself. By doing so, we lay the foundation for a future in which healing, empathy, and personal growth are not mere aspirations but central facets of our human experience.

This journey is far from over, and the road ahead offers both promise and challenges. But it's a road we needn't walk alone. It's a path that urges us to approach with openness, humility, and a heartfelt commitment to grasping the essence of our shared humanity. As we tread this path in unison, armed with wisdom, compassion, and a sense of purpose, we unlock transformative potentials that promise not just individual healing but the elevation of human experience as a whole. So here we are, poised and ready, on a path that beckons with the promise of discovery and the hope for a more compassionate world.

Cracking Psychedelic Code

Navigating through the intricate tapestry of consciousness and psychedelics is like traversing a complex computational landscape. Imagine your mind as a sophisticated computer, a harmonious blend of both hardware and software. Far from being a passive observer, your mind actively processes and encodes life's myriad experiences, transforming the abstract into the tangible. In this system, your consciousness functions as the software, directing the hardware—your brain—in a continuous dance of thoughts, emotions, and actions. This interplay creates the coded narrative that shapes our understanding of life.

Carrying this computational metaphor into the realm of religion can offer enlightening perspectives. Take, for example, Christianity's "Gospel of Thomas," a collection of sayings that emphasize the search for the kingdom within. In this context, Christ emerges not merely as a religious icon, but as the ultimate software update. He enriches both our internal operating system and our cosmic understanding. This viewpoint is not a departure from the text but rather an alignment with its core principle of self-discovery and internal wisdom.

Shifting our focus to Eastern philosophies like Buddhism, the mind is conceptualized as the root of all phenomena—a fertile canvas for the painting of life. But this is no ordinary canvas; it's a canvas imbued with enlightenment. Within Buddhism, the concept of the Buddha mind serves as the epitome of a decoded source code. It symbolizes a state of consciousness that has unraveled its own intricacies, facilitating a transcendent level of awareness. The Buddha mind represents a software that has not just been updated, but has been debugged and optimized to achieve a state of equilibrium and wisdom.

So, what then is the nature of the mind? Is it merely a mortal stream, forever susceptible to change and influence? Consider this: If the mind is a river, then consciousness is the ocean—limitless and eternal. Achieving peace requires a deep dive into this ocean of consciousness. To unlock your mind, you must let go—let go of judgments, preconceptions, and ego. A mind unburdened by these limitations is one that exists in a perpetual state of enlightenment, capable of cracking its own code.

For the past three decades of my life, I have been on a quest to crack the psychedelic code. The pursuit of extraordinary states of mind often boils down to two primary avenues: internally induced, or externally induced.

Both are capable of catapulting us into altered states, but

they do so through distinctly different mechanisms and produce different kinds of experiences.

One distinct difference between the two is the control and duration of the induced states. External methods, which typically involve ingesting or coming into contact with a natural or synthetic compound, usually come with a predetermined duration, set by the pharmacokinetics of the substance in use. In contrast, internal induction methods include activities like meditation. They offer more control, as the duration can often be sustained or terminated at will, providing a different level of agency over the experience.

My three decades of delving into these realms have taught me that the ultimate goal isn't necessarily about the means we employ, but about creating disruptions in our usual rhythms of life. For instance, my 21-day stay in a light-deprivation chamber served as a testament to the potency of internal methods. Afterall, although the chamber itself may be an external factor, its sole purpose is to facilitate the participants internal inductance.

Likewise, at the Monroe Institute, we found that manipulating sensory input and altering sleep patterns could induce extraordinary states. Practices like medical qigong, guided visualizations, and Sundo, an ancient Taoist technique, have also proven effective in this regard. The fascinating thing about these internal approaches is that they seem to produce shifts in our biochemistry, making them not entirely devoid of the influence of chemical compounds.

Contrast this with the direct chemical intervention of

psychedelics, which physically alter the brain's neurotransmitter systems via external stimulation. Depending on the substance, you might experience changes in serotonin receptors, as is the case with psilocybin, or broader effects on serotonin, dopamine, norepinephrine, and oxytocin as seen with MDMA. The immediacy and intensity of these experiences can be much higher compared to internal inductance, and this often allows for more rapid but also potentially overwhelming alterations in consciousness.

Exploring extraordinary states of mind is far from a risk-free endeavor, as I've observed through my own experiences in facilitating group retreats and light deprivation sessions. A lack of preparation or an improper environment can lead to unsettling, even harmful experiences. There have been instances where individuals emerged from the experience not rejuvenated, but bearing deeper emotional wounds. And in extreme cases, the consequences have even been fatal. This is a stern reminder that a facilitator's expertise and preparation are indispensable.

It's important to clarify that even under the most meticulous conditions, with the right mindset, setting, and calibrated use of substances, negative experiences can still arise. Yet, when managed appropriately, these uncomfortable moments can act as catalysts for deeper healing. The difference often lies in having a reliable support system in place—a network of experienced facilitators or caregivers that can help guide the internal journey and ensure a more constructive outcome.

Misguided intentions pose another set of risks. Pursuing these extraordinary states as a form of escapism or thrill-seeking, for instance, can not only result in unpleasant experiences but also reinforce detrimental patterns of behavior. The misuse of these potent states can essentially negate their potential benefits, turning them into yet another outlet for self-destructive habits.

The choice between internal and externally induced extraordinary states frequently hinges on individual preferences, the particular outcomes one seeks, and one's preparedness for navigating these landscapes. Both pathways offer unique advantages and limitations, and the most profound extraordinary states often lie in understanding the nuanced differences between them. Therefore, choosing between the two—or even integrating both—should be a well-considered decision, influenced by one's goals, experience, and respect for the transformative power these states hold.

Over the years, I've discovered that internal methods are not only incredibly effective but also safe pathways for journeying into extraordinary states of mind. These practices have become an indispensable part of my daily routine, each one offering its own unique gateway to altered consciousness.

In reading about my methods, I hope one thing will be made clear: You do not need access to a "magic" chemical, nor do you need funds for distant retreats. Anyone can alter their state of mind with shockingly simple practices.

First on the list is deep meditation. This cornerstone practice plunges me into a realm of heightened awareness and serenity by focusing on slowing down brainwave frequencies. The state it induces is a fertile sanctuary for introspection and revelation. To further augment this meditative state, I often integrate specialized breathing techniques that help me more deeply access these extraordinary mental landscapes.

Second on the list: sound therapy. Here, I engage in what I lovingly refer to as "tuning into the sound of the source." Whether it's binaural beats, the mystical reverberations of Tibetan singing bowls, or even the natural symphony of the wilderness, these auditory cues serve to harmonize brainwave frequencies. Intriguingly, I often employ shamanic music—recorded from my own transformative experiences—as a sonic catalyst, inviting me to re-experience the profound states of consciousness I've previously reached.

Third, I practice deep gratitude. Moving far beyond the pedestrian realm of gratitude journaling or basic reflective thinking, this method engulfs me in a transcendent state of gratitude. It's as if I tap into a universal reservoir of thankfulness, unleashing an emotional dynamism capable of initiating seismic shifts in mindset and guiding me into extraordinary realms of consciousness.

Fourth, and finally, I engage in guided visualization. Employing vivid mental canvases, this technique steers my consciousness into a variety of states or even otherworldly terrains. To heighten this immersive experience, I often weave sound therapy into the mix. These guided visual narratives can range from simplistic natural scenes to intricate, symbol-laden landscapes that encapsulate various facets of my own psyche.

The sheer beauty of these internal methods lies in their universal accessibility. They're cost-free, generally safe, and open to anyone willing to dedicate their time and energy. The key to their effectiveness is consistency; these are not fleeting, one-time ventures but sustained practices that accumulate in transformative power over time.

By folding these methods into the fabric of my daily existence, I find myself existing in what I like to call a "functional mode of consciousness." It's as if each passing moment is imbued with an intrinsic allure and significance, a state in which I find myself navigating daily life with enhanced presence, diminished stress, and a kind of existential clarity that emanates from the deeper strata of my awareness. This is an experience so profoundly enriching that I ardently wish for others to share in its bountiful rewards.

In a world grappling with increasing mental health challenges, ethical dilemmas, and widespread suffering, the exploration of extraordinary states of mind can offer more than just personal respite; it presents a path to potentially transformative global solutions. The focus shouldn't merely be on immediate therapeutic gains; instead, we should consider a broader, more profound impact. Imagine a scenario where a significant portion of humanity regularly accessed these non-ordinary states. The collective benefit could be a subtle yet potent healing of our shared mental landscape, effectively steering the human narrative toward a more constructive path.

Moreover, this isn't just lofty thinking; it's grounded in

emerging scientific disciplines like social neuroscience and quantum mechanics, which are beginning to demonstrate how individual shifts in consciousness can influence collective outcomes. We're not just isolated entities but interconnected parts of a greater whole. Even a small change in one individual can reverberate through the social fabric, subtly recalibrating the collective mindset.

Let's take a step back and examine the nature of these extraordinary states more closely. Engaging with them isn't just about experiencing something novel or intriguing. These states serve a very functional role; they create cognitive dissonance, breaking the monotony of our everyday mental patterns. Think of it as adjusting the contrast settings on a photograph. Suddenly, details previously hidden come to the forefront, allowing us to see our lives and the world around us with a newfound clarity.

This sharpened perspective is more than just personal insight; it can be profoundly transformative. It offers us a lens through which we can scrutinize not just the nuances of our individual existence but also the overarching themes of our collective journey. We begin to recognize the root causes of societal issues and, more importantly, visualize pathways to address them. Engaging in practices that access extraordinary states of mind is not merely a personal venture but a collective one. Through these experiences, we equip ourselves with the necessary insights to actively participate in creating a more conscious, compassionate, and sustainable world.

The impact of cultural and social variables on this journey cannot be overstated. Stigma, legal boundaries, and ethical considerations all frame our engagement with these extraordinary states. These external factors can either augment or hinder the effectiveness and safety of these practices, making it crucial to have a well-rounded understanding of the landscapes—both internal and external—that will influence the experience. Safety and harm reduction should always be at the forefront when venturing into these territories.

So, while the quest for extraordinary states of mind can be a transformative force both on a personal and collective level, it's not a journey to be undertaken lightly. The complexities and potential risks necessitate a nuanced approach. Preparation, intentionality, and a deep respect for the power and sanctity of these states are essential preconditions for anyone looking to navigate this transformative terrain successfully.

Witnessing the spectrum of human life, from the innocence of newborns to the vulnerability of the elderly, can change the sense through which we experience the world. These stages of life are like the rising and setting sun—each has its beauty and challenges. But remember, the sun hasn't vanished; it's just shifted location. Similarly, our true selves are not confined to the cycle of birth and death; we are essence, consciousness, eternal source code (EOS).

To those who find themselves struggling to reach these extraordinary states of mind, let me impart this: attaining EOS is fundamentally an intrinsic capability, as innate to us as the act of breathing. You don't have to "learn" how to breathe; it's a spontaneous function, an inherent part of your being. The same goes for accessing extraordinary states—it's a quality you were born with, but may have been suppressed or ignored due to societal conditioning or personal apprehensions.

I understand that saying this is one thing, while experiencing it can be another story. The challenge often lies in surrendering control and letting go, in relinquishing our grip on the 'known' to embrace the 'unknown.' For some, this comes naturally, as though they've discovered the "right password" to log into this expanded state of awareness. For others, it requires dedicated practice, a continual process of internal alignment and refinement.

So, if you find yourself struggling, remember that both pathways—the spontaneous and the cultivated—are valid routes to the extraordinary. Open yourself up to the possibilities, and you'll find that these extraordinary states of mind are not as elusive as they might seem. All it takes is granting yourself the permission to explore, to step beyond your comfort zones, and to venture into the uncharted realms of consciousness.

Acknowledgements

To the silent whispers of my heart and the dreams that echoed in the deepest corridors of my mind, this journey towards "The Exploratory Mind, Rewiring Sentience" was a dance of destiny and diligence. At the crux of this voyage stood the indomitable spirits of Dr. Richard Louis Miller, Dr. Rick Doblin, Dr. Dennis McKenna, Dr. Stanislav Grof, Dr. Michael and Annie Mithoefer, Bruce Poulter, Marcela Ot'alora, and numerous other luminaries in the consciousness and psychedelics science community.

An integral part of this expedition has been the wisdom of Dr. David Morehouse, Joe McMoneagle, and the profound insights from The Monroe Institute and my cherished remote viewing community. My gratitude stretches out to Jorge Luis Delgado, MaryAnn and Theron Male for guiding my journey through the mystical Andean landscapes. To Charlotte, a dear friend whose presence has been an anchor in navigating the realms of the unseen, I owe a debt of deep gratitude.

HeartMath™ provided the foundational steps in understanding the profound science of the heart, and their teachings have been pivotal in molding my perspective. A special acknowledgment to His Holiness the Dalai Lama and all the Geshe whose teachings of loving compassion resonate profoundly and echo throughout the world.

My stint as a psychedelic psychotherapist in Australia, under the aegis of MAPS Training at the Psychedelic Lab at Monash University, has been an enlightening experience. It unveiled a community of clinical and scientific healers, where every interaction was an epiphany, reshaping my understanding and reinforcing the urge to convey this profound narrative through a blend of scientific research and personal revelations.

To the elders, visionaries, and mentors in the medical, scientific, and mystic realms, your teachings and insights have been the backbone of this endeavor. My heart swells with gratitude for the knowledge you have shared and the paths you have illuminated.

In penning this work, my hope soars high — a hope that each page and every word contributes to healing humanity, nurturing souls, and fostering a collective evolution, one mindful thought at a time. To everyone who has been a part of this transformative journey, I am eternally thankful.

Made in the USA
Monee, IL
03 April 2024